Afghanistan

Afghanistan

BY RUTH BJORKLUND

Enchantment of the World™
Second Series

CHILDREN'S PRESS®

An Imprint of Scholastic Inc.

Frontispiece: **Aimaq girl**

Consultant: M. Asef Mehry, M.Ed. Southern Illinois University Carbondale & Oversight Committee member of Afghanistan Fulbright Association

Please note: All statistics are as up-to-date as possible at the time of publication.

Book production by The Design Lab

Library of Congress Cataloging-in-Publication Data
Names: Bjorklund, Ruth, author.
Title: Afghanistan / by Ruth Bjorklund.
Description: New York, NY : Children's Press, an imprint of Scholastic Inc., [2018] |
    Series: Enchantment of the world | Includes bibliographical references and index.
Identifiers: LCCN 2017025769 | ISBN 9780531235874 (library binding)
Subjects: LCSH: Afghanistan—Juvenile literature.
Classification: LCC DS351.5 .B54 2018 | DDC 958.1—dc23
LC record available at https://lccn.loc.gov/2017025769

Scholastic Inc., 557 Broadway, New York, NY 10012

1 2 3 4 5 6 7 8 9 10 R 27 26 25 24 23 22 21 20 19 18

Blue Mosque, Mazar-i-Sharif

Contents

Left to right: **Flying kites, family, cashmere goats, carrying wood, eating lunch**

CHAPTER 1

Welcome Home

KHALID WOKE EARLY AND GOT READY FOR SCHOOL. He dressed and washed and joined his parents to pray. They arranged their prayer rugs side by side, facing southwest. Every morning, they begin by standing and reciting "*Allahu Akbar*," meaning "God is great." As their prayer continues, they kneel and lower their foreheads to the floor. Khalid and his family are Muslims, followers of the religion Islam. Like other Muslims, they pray five times a day, always in the direction of Mecca, Saudi Arabia, birthplace of the Prophet Muhammad.

Khalid lives in Afghanistan, a rugged country in south-central Asia. Khalid's mother, a teacher, left the house before him. She needed to prepare before her students arrived. His father works in business exporting cotton to Pakistan. He offered Khalid a ride to school, but Khalid wanted to walk. His city, Jalalabad, is one of the most beautiful cities in

Opposite: **Children play in the courtyard of their home in Kabul.**

Afghanistan. Although temperatures in summer can be more than 100 degrees Fahrenheit (38 degrees Celsius), it was a warm spring day, and gardens and parks were lush green and flowers bloomed, scenting the air.

Khalid is in his first year of high school, which is very different from elementary school. Elementary schools are overcrowded. Khalid went to school on the second shift, in

A boy sells bread at a market in Mazar-i-Sharif.

the afternoon. He shared a desk and textbooks with another student. Most of the students who went to school for the morning shift worked in the afternoon. Some helped in the family business, such as a shop or workshop making pottery. Some set up small homemade stands on the side of the road to sell bread or fruits. Khalid did not have to work, and he knows that he is fortunate to have parents with good jobs who can afford to send him to school. He has two older brothers, both now in college, one studying engineering at Nangarhar University and the other at medical school in Kabul, the nation's capital.

Unemployment is high in Afghanistan, with sometimes almost 40 percent of workers unable to find jobs. But his brothers will have no trouble finding work once they graduate. Afghanistan is in dire need of doctors, engineers, and tradespeople. The country has been living with terrorism and war for decades. Beginning in the 1980s, many professionals—health care workers, engineers, and teachers—fled the country after it was invaded by the Soviet Union. Now, progress and stability are slowly emerging. Professionals are returning, and people are being educated. Years of war brought countless casualties, with too few health care workers to care for them. Bombs, tanks, and rockets continue to blow up roads, bridges, and buildings. It will take many engineers and construction workers to rebuild cities and towns.

Beyond rebuilding, the government wants to improve lives. Many Afghans live in rural villages and remote mountains and valleys. Village life is about god, family, and friends. Houses are humble, and most people grow their own fruits and vegetables

An Afghan woman works at an internet TV company. A growing number of media companies have opened in Afghanistan in recent years.

and raise their own chickens and livestock. Many of these communities have no electricity or freshwater wells. There are too few schools and often no computers. Many of these problems also exist in cities, which are rapidly becoming overcrowded.

When Khalid returned home after school, he was in for a surprise. His Uncle Aziz and Aunt Mina and four cousins stood in the front of the house, in the *hujra*, or guest room. He had not seen his relatives for more than twelve years. Khalid had never even met his cousins. Aziz and Mina and their children had been refugees in Pakistan for many years. They had joined the hundreds of thousands of Afghans who fled their villages when they were attacked. Some refugees made new lives in Pakistan, and others lived in refugee camps. Khalid's uncle, once a successful wheat farmer, worked as a laborer in Pakistan. Now, Pakistan is forcing refugees to return to Afghanistan. But when the refugees arrive, most of their former life is gone—their homes, farms, and villages have been destroyed. Friends and families have moved or been killed. Many refugees choose to move to cities, but there are not enough jobs or housing.

When Khalid's parents returned home, they were equally surprised to see their relatives. No Afghan turns a visitor away, especially a family member. So they welcomed the family and invited them to stay. Khalid's parents knew that the two families could not permanently live together. After a discussion, Aziz decided to move the family to Kabul and look for a job. His daughter, Maryam, however, would stay with Khalid's family, where she could get a good education.

When the day came for them to leave for Kabul, Khalid's parents took them to the bus station. The drive to Kabul is not long, but it is harrowing. Cars and buses scream around the one-lane road, passing each other on blind curves. But the scenery is spectacular—sharp rocky cliffs tower above the Kabul River valley. The massive snow-capped Hindu Kush mountains fill the horizon.

The road between Jalalabad and Kabul is near the Khyber Pass, one of the main border crossings to Pakistan, and a headquarters for terrorist groups. One group, the Taliban, had once governed Afghanistan with harsh Islamic law. They forbade girls from going to school and ordered women to cover themselves in burkas—long robes that cover the body and face. They told men how to dress as well and forced young men into joining their rebel movement, and destroyed villages and farms if people resisted. Another terrorist group, the Islamic State (often called ISIS), operates in many countries.

Both groups are surging in Afghanistan, and even in areas where people once felt safe from attack, many now fear for their lives and property. Jalalabad and Kabul are relatively safe and well guarded, but attacks happen. Yet, the cities are bustling with hopeful activity—there are shops, museums, restaurants, schools, and parks that draw people out into the community.

The night after Aziz and his other relatives left, Khalid told Maryam that he had joined the Afghan scouts. Young Afghan people have been scouting for more than seventy-five years. Khalid's father had once been a scout, enjoying activities such as camping and hiking. But after the Soviet-

Trucks make their way along narrow roads in northeastern Afghanistan. The roads through Afghanistan's rugged mountains can be treacherous.

backed communist regime gained control of Afghanistan in the 1970s, they forced scouts into supporting communism and expected them to act as a volunteer police force in villages. Later, when the Taliban came to power, mullahs, or teachers of Islamic law, forbade scouts from sitting around a campfire, calling it fire worship. Most scoutmasters quit, and with them went the scouts. Scouts today focus on helping people in need, volunteering in hospitals, and tutoring younger students.

Maryam decided she wanted to help serve her country and would join the scouts, too. Her hero is Khatool Mohammadzai, a paratrooper and the first female general in the Afghan army. Many conservative Afghans discriminate against women and girls. But women, and the men who support equal rights, are beginning to speak out. General Mohammadzai encourages the fight for equal rights, saying, "Afghan men and women are the wings of one bird."

CHAPTER 2

A Rugged Land

ONG AGO, WHEN DINOSAURS LIVED, THE LAND that is Afghanistan was a marshy coastline along an ocean. South of this ocean was a huge mass of land. Over eons, part of this mass began pulling away from the rest. Slowly, it moved north until it collided with what is now Afghanistan. The land from the south—the Indian subcontinent—slowly pushed under the other land in Asia. As the landmasses collided, the rocky area was pushed upward, forming some of the world's tallest and most forbidding mountains. These mountain ranges crisscross northeastern and central Afghanistan. The country is bordered by China, Tajikistan, Uzbekistan, and Turkmenistan to the north and Iran to the west. Afghanistan shares its long eastern border with Pakistan.

Opposite: **Much of northern Afghanistan is marked by jagged ridges.**

Afghanistan's Geographic Features

Highest Elevation: Mount Nowshakh 24,580 feet (7,492 m) above sea level

Lowest Elevation: Amu Darya riverbed, 846 feet (258 m) above sea level

Greatest Distance East to West: About 770 miles (1,240 km)

Greatest Distance North to South: About 350 miles (565 km)

Area: 251,827 square miles (652,230 sq km)

Longest River Entirely Within Afghanistan: Helmand River, about 715 miles (1,150 km)

Highest Recorded Temperature: 122°F (50°C) in Farah, August 2009

Lowest Recorded Temperature: −62°F (−52°C) in Shahrak, January 1964

Average Annual Precipitation: 12 inches (30 cm)

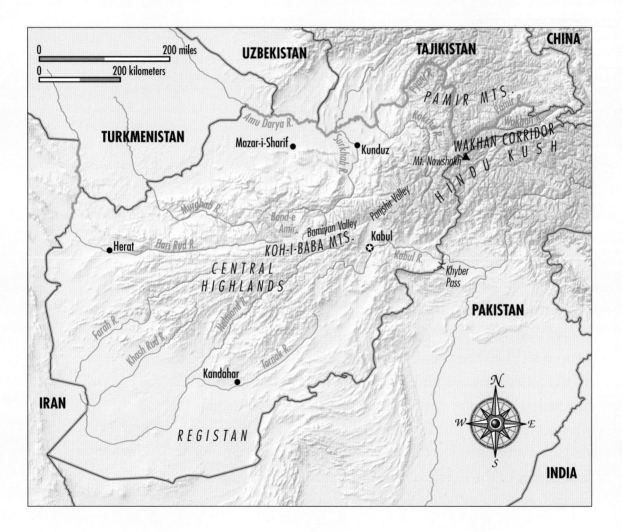

Ali's Dragon

Long ago in the central highlands, a volcano exploded, releasing water and lava at the same time. The lava first created an 820-foot-long (250 m) rock ridge. But as each new spurt of lava erupted into the air, the bursting shoots of water quickly cooled it. The water split the rock formation down the middle. Inside the split, large vertical rock spines formed, resembling ribs. As more lava spewed upward, the water froze it in place, creating tall spikes along the length of the rock. As the flow of lava slowed, it grew into a thick ball. The water captured the lava ball and formed it into a giant "head" about 32 feet (10 m) long and 25 feet (8 m) wide.

The ball has an indentation, resembling an eye. Atop the ball, a thick, hornlike spike rises upward. To many people who have seen this spectacular work of nature, it looks like a dragon.

Local legend has it that Hazrat Ali, the son-in-law of the Muslim Prophet Muhammad, fought and slayed the dragon in defense of the people of the Bamiyan Valley. It was his valiant sword that split the dragon down the middle.

A flow of white, pasty water continues today to seep out of the "eye" in the dragon's head. People say the drips of water are the dragon's tears of shame.

Central Highlands

Afghanistan's mountainous terrain marches more than 500 miles (800 kilometers) from the far northeast across the central highlands to the deserts of the southwestern plateau. The central highlands cover almost two-thirds of the country. The largest of the mountain ranges in the highlands is the Hindu Kush. Several peaks rise more than 20,000 feet (6,100 meters) in the northeastern section of the Hindu Kush, including the highest peak in Afghanistan, Nowshakh, which reaches 24,580 feet (7,492 m). Deep, narrow valleys slice through the steep, nearly treeless mountains. The peaks are capped by glaciers and receive more precipitation, in the form of snow, than elsewhere in the country. Other mountain ranges include the Koh-i-Baba and the Pamirs, a branch of the Himalayas. These mighty mountains are often referred to as the Roof of the World.

Because of Afghanistan's arid climate, farms tend to be located along rivers.

In the extreme northeast of the central highlands is the Wakhan Corridor, which extends 220 miles (354 km) between Tajikistan and Pakistan toward China. It is a remote finger of land where jagged, glacier-capped mountains surround high valleys. For centuries, nomadic herders have grazed yaks and sheep and grown crops of barley and wheat in the region. The Pamir and Wakhan Rivers flow across the high valleys to join the Pyanj River. The beautiful Pyanj Valley is famous for its fruit orchards, mainly grapes and mulberries.

The Hindu Kush is the source of Afghanistan's most important rivers, such as the Amu Darya, Hari Rud, Kabul, and Helmand Rivers. The Amu Darya is the only river in Afghanistan that is largely navigable. The Hari Rud River flows north and west and provides irrigation for farms and pasturelands. The Kabul River's dams provide hydroelectric power to the country's two largest cities. The Helmand River is the longest river to flow entirely within Afghanistan.

The Bamiyan Valley, west of the capital city of Kabul in the central highlands, is ringed by dramatic limestone cliffs and the Hindu Kush and Koh-i-Baba mountain ranges. The valley is fertile and lush and features six pure, dark blue lakes called the Band-e Amir. They are deep craters of former volcanoes and the site of Afghanistan's first national park.

A man rides a donkey past one of the bright blue Band-e Amir lakes. The lakes have been protected as Afghanistan's first national park.

North and South

The northern plains are the most fertile region in Afghanistan. Rolling hills and grasslands support a wide variety of agriculture and livestock. This type of grassland region, usually located between desert and forest, is called steppe. If more rain fell on the steppe, the steppe would grow trees and become forest. If less rain fell, the steppe would become desert. The Afghan steppe receives only about 17 inches (43 centimeters) of rain a year. Although it is dry, the region has wide swaths of greenery, because irrigation systems supply water to farms and pastures.

The Song of the Desert

Travelers crossing the deserts of Afghanistan are often stunned to hear mysterious musical noises with no obvious source. Some ancient travelers believed the noises were made by evil spirits.

Singing sand dunes are a rare phenomenon—there are only about forty in the world. Two singing dune formations, Reg-i-Ruwan and Kwachau, are in southern Afghanistan.

A number of elements must be present to produce singing sands. First, the sand dunes must be tall and steep. Winds must be strong enough to batter the grains of sand and make them tiny, perfectly round, and equal in size. There must be almost no humidity. The sounds are formed when the sand is disturbed, usually by winds. Small avalanches of the topmost layer of sand tumble down the slopes of the dunes. The grains bump into each other and bounce back off, causing vibrations. Afghanistan's singing sands are quite loud and do actually produce musical notes.

Southern Afghanistan is mostly an arid, treeless landscape of high plateaus, cliffs, caves, and desert. The largest desert is the Registan in the southwest. The area is hot and dry. During the summer, north winds send blinding twisters of sand across the dunes. Although the southeast is also dry, heavy spring winds sometimes carry clouds thick with moisture up from the Arabian Sea, producing flooding rains.

Children use water containers as sleds after a snowstorm in Kabul. Snow is common in the city from December through February.

Hot and Cold

Climate, like all else in Afghanistan, is affected by the presence of mountains. Afghanistan's climate is extreme. Winter and summer temperatures vary dramatically. Southern deserts average 95°F (35°C) in summer, while the central high-

A man walks through a sandstorm south of Kabul. In a sandstorm, it is sometimes impossible to see more than a few feet in any direction.

lands average a chilly 5°F (–15°C) in winter. Rainfall, too, is affected by the mountains. Clouds carrying rain from the ocean are mostly blocked by the high peaks, so little rain or snow falls in Afghanistan. The country overall averages just 12 inches (30 cm) of precipitation a year, mostly in the northeast, where mountain areas can receive as much as 40 inches (100 cm) of snow. Desert regions receive less than 4 inches (10 cm) of rain a year. In summer, cooling winds coming from snowcapped peaks bring relief from the sweltering heat. However, summer winds can also bring huge sandstorms that blast across the southern desert.

A Look at Afghan Cities

Kabul, the capital city, has a population of nearly 3.6 million people, making it by far the largest city in the nation.

Kandahar (below) is Afghanistan's second-largest city with an estimated population of 491,500 people. Nearly all residents belong to the Pashtun ethnic group. The city houses treasured shrines and mixes ancient architecture with new. Kandahar is a vital communications and transportation hub for southern Afghanistan. It is also a center of food processing and is an important area for making wool textiles.

Herat is Afghanistan's third-largest city, home to about 436,000 people. In the fifteenth century, Herat was a great trading center located along major trade routes between Europe, Arabia, and Asia. As caravans

of riches passed through, the city blossomed into a cultural center, where artists, poets, and craftspeople thrived. Several shrines around the city are devoted to their memory and accomplishments. The city's most notable monument is the Citadel, a fortress that has been destroyed and rebuilt many times through the centuries. Herat's Friday Mosque (above) is considered one of the most beautiful mosques in central Asia.

Mazar-i-Sharif, home to about 370,000 people, is the trading hub of northern Afghanistan. It lies in an agricultural valley where a variety of fruits, vegetables, and grains are grown. People there also raise livestock, such as the prized Karakul sheep. At the heart of the city stands the elegant Blue Mosque, or the Tomb of Hazrat Ali, a Shi'a Muslim holy man.

CHAPTER 3

Natural Riches

AS DRY AND MOUNTAINOUS AS AFGHANISTAN is, it is surprisingly rich in plant and animal species. More than two thousand plant species can be found in the country. More than 20 percent of them are endemic, meaning that they are found nowhere else on the planet.

Afghanistan is one of eight parts of the world where wild plants were first developed into crops. Centuries ago, early farmers planted wild plants and tended to their growth. They chose native plants that would be the hardiest and most nutritious, including wheat, peas, lentils, sesame, onions, garlic, spinach, carrots, pistachios, pears, melons, almonds, walnuts, grapes, and apples.

Opposite: **Many colorful flowers grow well in Afghanistan's cool, arid mountains and steppes.**

A man carries a load of firewood along a road in Kandahar. Many Afghans rely on wood for heating and cooking.

Trees

Only 2 percent of Afghanistan is forested. Nearly all trees are found in the river valleys and foothills. Higher in the mountains are evergreens, such as pine, spruce, and cedar. Farther down the slopes are trees, such as oak, poplar, and maple. The river valleys support the largest variety of trees—wild hazelnuts, walnuts, almonds, and pistachios. In the east, where heavy rain is sometimes common, forests produce flowering rhododendrons, locusts, and mulberries. Thirty years ago, there were far more trees in Afghanistan than there are now. Years of war destroyed many treed areas. Trees are also cut for building construction, fuel, and heat. Trees with valuable woods such as walnut and oak are cut and smuggled out of the country. The government is making an effort to conserve forested areas and prevent smuggling.

All-Purpose Bush

Wormwood, a type of sagebrush, is a low-growing, woody bush that Afghans use for many different purposes. In fall and winter, Afghans on the steppe gather great armloads of wormwood. The root of the plant burns hot and slow and is one of the best sources of fuel for cooking and heating. Oil produced by the plant is heavily scented and gives extra flavor to cooked foods, especially bread. Wormwood is also used for making brooms.

Scrub and Grasses

Few trees grow on the steppe of the northern plains. Steppe grasses hold the soil in place and provide food for grazing livestock. Grasses include goat grass, salt grass, yellow bluestem, and meadow foxtail. Steppe grasses also produce seeds that are used to flavor food, such as caraway, cumin, coriander, and licorice. Scrub brush plants include camel thorn, juniper, locoweed, mimosa, glasswort, and sagebrush.

Flowers

After the snow melts or the spring rains fall, Afghanistan comes alive for a brief time with the colors of thousands of different species of flowering plants. Among them are blossoming peas, thistles, lilies, and irises. Wild herbs are abundant, including marjoram, thyme, mint, and oregano. The tulip, which flourishes in valleys, originated in the Pamirs and the Hindu Kush, and is the national flower of Afghanistan. Several varieties of

Snow leopards live high in the mountains of Afghanistan and other Asian countries. They are carnivores, eating only meat. They prey on whatever animals they encounter, including ibex, wild goats, and hares.

fragrant flowers bloom after the spring rains in southeastern Afghanistan, including roses, honeysuckles, and gooseberries.

Mammals

Afghanistan is home to hundreds of species of mammals, from common creatures such as hares, bats, and dormice to rare species such as snow leopards, ibex, and rhesus macaques. Most animals that live in the steppe are grazing animals that feed on wild grasses, although some, like the corsac fox and the striped hyena, will eat prey. Animals found on the steppe include rabbits, mice, gazelle, deer, marmots, hedgehogs, mongooses, and porcupines. Scientists were surprised to discover a small herd of steppe-dwelling Bactrian deer, long thought extinct, in Afghanistan.

Saiga Antelope

The saiga antelope is easily identifiable by the large hump on its nose. This animal has many adaptations that help it survive in its steppe environment. The thick covering over the nose is flexible and inflatable. In summer, the antelope enlarges the hump to filter out sand. In winter, it inflates the hump to help warm cold air. Living on the open steppe, the saiga antelope's swift legs and sharp eyesight help it escape predators. Its fur also blends in with the colors of the seasons—sand-colored in summer and white in winter—helping it to hide.

Saiga antelopes are also known for their lengthy migrations. After the antelope herds gather to mate, the males separate and form one large herd and migrate to northern feeding grounds. After the females give birth to their calves, they too form a herd, often several thousand strong. The females and calves catch up to the males, and together the herds travel 50 to 70 miles a day (80 to 110 km) to reach their feeding grounds. Even when not migrating, saiga antelopes are on the move. They may walk 20 miles (30 km) a day while grazing with their heads down and their humped noses snuffling to filter out dust.

Despite all its survival adaptations, the saiga antelope is critically endangered. The animals are often hunted for food. Additionally, their habitat is increasingly being taken over by agricultural activity.

Steppe animals have adapted to fit into their environment in many ways. Larger animals, such as gazelle and antelope, use their speed to run from predators. Smaller animals escape from predators by digging burrows or hiding in rocky crevices.

The Wakhan Corridor in northeastern Afghanistan is home to a wide variety of wildlife. The region is so remote that dozens of rare animal species have been able to survive. The rare Marco Polo sheep, for example, is the world's largest sheep. Its large horns are highly prized for use in Chinese folk medicine, as are the long, spiraling horns of the markhor, a rare wild goat. Poachers, people who hunt illegally, kill the animals for their horns and sell them at high prices.

Mountain dwellers consider the snow leopard a dangerous pest. The leopards prey on sheep, goats, and yaks. Though the snow leopard is endangered worldwide, and it is illegal to hunt these creatures, some herders kill the leopards if they believe their herds are threatened. Additionally, there are poachers who sell the highly desired leopard skins to collectors.

Marco Polo sheep are notable for their long horns that point directly away from their heads. They are the longest horns of any sheep, with some reaching 6 feet (1.8 m) in length.

Birds, Reptiles, Fish, and Amphibians

The central highlands are home to hundreds of species of birds, although most are migrants stopping over on their journey between summer and winter feeding grounds. Many of them, such as bitterns, herons, ducks, flamingos, and the threatened Siberian cranes, are found in the Band-e Amir lakes region and other wetlands. Songbirds, buzzards, partridges, eagles, and falcons can be found throughout the steppe.

Fish such as trout and carp thrive in Afghanistan's lakes and streams. Conservationists are concerned about wetland wildlife, however, because too much water is being drained off for farming and too many fish are being caught.

Most of Afghanistan is too dry for amphibians, but some species of frogs and toads, such as the skittering frog and the Iranian earless toad, do well in the wetlands. On the other hand, lizards, snakes, and other reptiles thrive in the steppe and desert areas. One of the most impressive reptiles is the desert monitor, which can grow 6.5 feet (2 m) long. The lizard uses venom to capture and subdue its prey, including mice, birds, and other lizards, such as geckos. Geckos are also prey for poisonous scorpions, tarantulas, centipedes, and camel spiders.

Siberian cranes migrate south each winter from the Arctic regions of northern Russia. They use their long bills to forage for food in lakes and marshes.

The Russian tortoise can pull its head all the way inside its shell to protect itself.

Afghanistan is home to more than twenty-five species of snakes. Two of the most poisonous are the Central Asian pit viper and the Oxus cobra. The pit viper strikes quickly. Its venom has no antidote, and most victims die. The Oxus cobra lurks in caves and tree hollows, and under rocks. Before striking, the cobra raises its upper body and puffs out its hood. Its venom constricts the victims' airways, choking off the air supply. A few species of tortoise are found in Afghanistan. Russian tortoises are common and are often caught and sold as pets.

Conservation

Afghanistan's National Environmental Protection Agency, along with many foreign environmental groups, is working to protect the nation's many rare species. It is no small task, as war has disrupted the environment. In addition, people living with war and poverty often rely on food they have hunted or fished. However, many of Afghanistan's conservation efforts have been successful, as demonstrated by the growing number of Bactrian deer and the establishment of new national parks and wildlife refuges.

The Second National Park

In 2014, the director of Afghanistan's National Environmental Protection Agency, Prince Mustafa Zaher, designated the Wakhan Corridor as Afghanistan's second national park. He called it "one of the last truly wild places on the planet." The park protects mountains, valleys, and alpine grasslands from development. Although the region is too harsh and isolated to be harmed by farming, logging, or mining, many areas have been damaged by overgrazing.

The park plays a crucial role in protecting endangered animals, as well as hundreds of other species. Unlike most national parks, however, that are not residential, the Afghan government allows about 15,000 people—ethnic Wakhis and Kyrgyz herders—to live within the park. They are restricted from herding in some areas, especially the rocky territory of the snow leopard. In return for being able to maintain their traditional lifestyle, the herders are expected to help rangers manage the park and protect the animals.

CHAPTER 4

A Long March

THOUSANDS OF YEARS AGO, CIVILIZATIONS developed in Europe, Asia, India, Arabia, and Persia. Afghanistan was surrounded by these civilizations and became a crossroads for trade and a target for conquest. Afghanistan's heritage is one of riches and war. Traders led caravans across the rugged landscape carrying valuable goods and exciting new ideas. Meanwhile, conquering armies invaded, raiding natural resources and taking over governments.

Opposite: **This two-thousand-year-old Afghani earring depicts a king with two dragons.**

Cave Dwellers

More than one hundred thousand years ago, early humans left behind stone tools in various sites in northern and central Afghanistan. Among the tools scientists have found are stone cleavers, choppers, and axes. In about 35,000 BCE, nomadic herders lived in rock shelters at Kara Kamar, in the Hindu Kush mountains. Archaeologists digging in the mud there found a variety of tools and weapons made of flint. Near

This ancient stone figure is thought to be a fertility goddess. It was made about four thousand years ago.

Mazar-i-Sharif, scientists uncovered a limestone pebble with a carving of a human face, one of the earliest images of a human face ever discovered. The carving was created around 18,000 BCE. Several thousand years later, people in Afghanistan began forming some of the world's first permanent settlements, farming wild crops such as wheat, and domesticating sheep and goats.

Early Settlements

The Bronze Age occurred in Afghanistan between 5500 BCE and 2900 BCE. It was a time of major changes in the region. People used new materials such as bronze, copper, and glass to make tools and household goods. The people also made social and cultural advances. They decorated pottery with geometric patterns and paintings of plants and animals. They carved and painted jewelry made from beads, bones, clay, metal, and colored stones. People hoping for healthy harvests sculpted clay figurines of fertility symbols such as goddesses and deer. Agriculture became the way of life.

Near the end of the Bronze Age, an advanced society known as the Indus Valley Civilization developed across parts of what are now India, Pakistan, and Afghanistan. Its people constructed houses and public buildings of brick and stone. They built drainage and water systems, and cobblestone roads and bridges. They developed a written script and a system of weights and measures used for trading. Traders crossed Afghanistan to reach the major Indus Valley cities. Caravans carried pottery, beads, incense, spices, grains, nuts, precious metals, and gemstones such as turquoise, lapis lazuli, rubies, and pearls. Cities along the trade routes flourished. Shortughai, near the Amu Darya river where lapis lazuli was mined, was Afghanistan's leading Indus Valley trading center.

The people of the Indus Valley Civilization constructed two large cities and many towns. They made many advancements, including building covered drainage systems.

Migrants and Conquests

By 1500 BCE, the Indus Valley Civilization was failing. Taking its place was an invading group called the Aryans. The invaders conquered much of the region, naming it Ariana and ruling for more than a thousand years.

Beginning around 600 BCE, another ancient empire, the Bactrian, occupied what is now northern Afghanistan, Uzbekistan, and Tajikistan. Its capital was the Afghan city of

A drinking cup from the Bactrian Empire. The Bactrian people made goods from gold, silver, and other precious materials.

Balkh. The city was surrounded by gold, silver, and lapis lazuli mining deposits and became a wealthy trading hub.

Balkh was later an important cultural center for the Achaemenid and Macedonian Empires. In 540 BCE, when Persian ruler Cyrus the Great conquered Ariana, his Achaemenid Empire became one of the largest empires in the history of the world. Cyrus the Great allowed the territories he captured to keep their traditions. He introduced a system of regional governments headed by a strong central government. The government introduced an official language that made it easier to build roads and communication networks between towns and cities. Achaemenid rule in Afghanistan lasted only two hundred years, but its system of government inspired many future leaders.

In distant Macedonia, a young Greek military commander known as Alexander the Great was determined to destroy the Achaemenid Empire. In 330 BCE, he began attacking Afghanistan from the south. His troops eventually captured Herat and Kandahar. As winter set in and Alexander's armies pressed north, they were overwhelmed by the bitter cold and rugged terrain. They came upon Balkh and demanded food

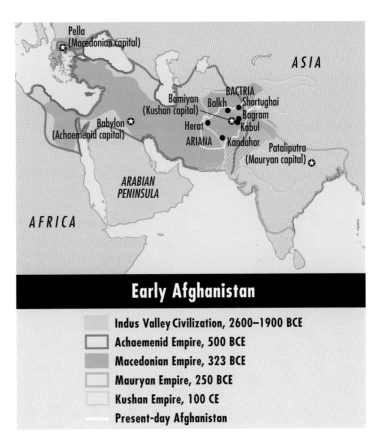

Early Afghanistan

Indus Valley Civilization, 2600–1900 BCE
Achaemenid Empire, 500 BCE
Macedonian Empire, 323 BCE
Mauryan Empire, 250 BCE
Kushan Empire, 100 CE
Present-day Afghanistan

and shelter for the winter. The city's beauty and prosperity impressed Alexander, so before marching on toward further conquests, he left behind soldiers with orders to build forts and housing. He assigned tradespeople, architects, doctors, artisans, and scholars to settle in Balkh. The Macedonians introduced Greek food, ceremonies, language, and culture to the Bactrians. They built Greek temples, marketplaces, and theaters.

Alexander died young, leaving no heir, so the Macedonian Empire fell into disarray and was divided up. Afghan groups in the south took advantage of the changes and mounted several rebellions. Meanwhile, the Mauryan dynasty of India had spread toward Afghanistan. Afghan rulers decided it was better to give up southern Afghanistan than to defend it. Kandahar and southeastern Afghanistan were sold to the Mauryan dynasty for gold and five hundred war elephants.

Ashoka, the grandson of the founder of the Mauryan dynasty, took the throne in 268 BCE. He was a brutal and brilliant battle strategist and eventually conquered most of India and the Hindu Kush region of Afghanistan. He ruled with strict law and cruel punishment. But midway through his reign, he had a change of heart and converted to Buddhism, a peaceful religion. After his death, the Mauryan dynasty came to an end, and the realm became vulnerable to other armies.

The Kushans

Afghanistan's neighbor China was home to several different groups, including the Kushans. Around 150 BCE, the Kushans attacked Bactria and, by doing so, created an empire. The Kushans ruled for three hundred years and brought immense changes to the region.

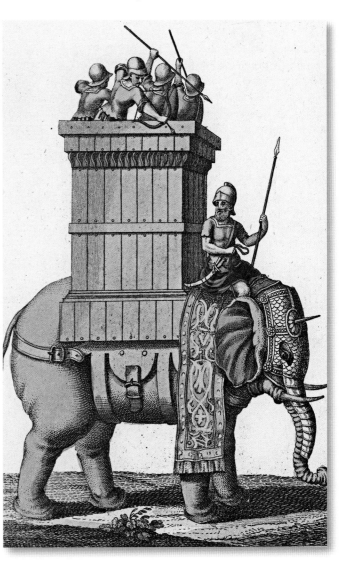

Indian armies were the first to use war elephants. Only the head and trunk of the powerful beast was armored.

The Kushans were important participants in trade along the Silk Road. The Silk Road was the name given to a series of rugged overland trails that connected East Asia and India to Persia, Arabia, Africa, and Europe. Europeans sent their merchants east to trade wool, colored glass, horses, and wine. In return, China traded silk, porcelain, and lacquerware. India

Camel caravans carried valuable goods back and forth across Asia on the Silk Road. The route went all the way from China to the Mediterranean Sea.

The Treasures of Bagram

Bagram, north of Kabul, was the wealthy summer palace of the Kushan royalty. The city was surrounded by a high brick wall and guard towers. Shops, food markets, lodging, and workshops lined the main street. In the 1930s, a team of French archaeologists unearthed a sealed vault and found a vast treasure trove of ancient artifacts dating back to the era of the Silk Road. Their discoveries included luxury items such as Roman bronze statuettes, intricately carved Indian ivories, Egyptian painted glass, Greek clay ornaments, and Chinese lacquerware.

Archaeologists believe that the luxury goods were left behind when an invading army raided the Kushan palace. There was too much treasure for the fleeing Kushans to carry so they bricked over a storeroom's entrance to hide their precious cache from their enemies.

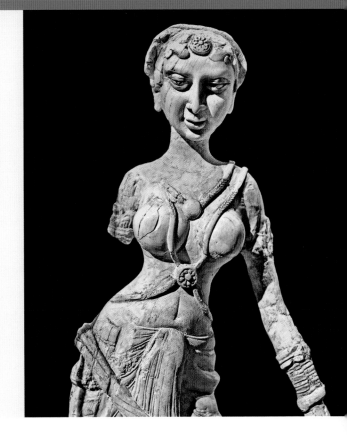

supplied ivory, perfume, beads, gems, and dyed cotton cloth. Southeast Asia and the East Indies offered up spices, such as cinnamon and clove, incense, and tea. Persia traded woven carpets, and Arabia and Africa traded ivory, glass, gold, and exotic animal feathers and fur.

The traders led caravans of camels and worked in relays. They crisscrossed Afghanistan and made stopovers to rest, trade, and pass along their goods to the next group of traders. The Kushans provided security and protection for the camel caravans along the route. Several Kushan cities on the Silk Road flourished as trading centers, especially Balkh. The Kushans could speak and write Greek, a language familiar to many European traders. They also minted gold coins with images of Greek gods and royalty, which the European traders easily accepted as payment for goods.

Invasions

When the Kushan Empire weakened, Afghanistan broke up into many small kingdoms, which were vulnerable to attack. The first to invade was the Persian Sasanian Empire, which at its height included what is now Iran, Central Asia, Turkey, India, and many parts of the Middle East. The Sasanians brought classical Persian art, literature, and music to Afghanistan. Although the Sasanians had conquered much of Afghanistan, the Kushans and the small Afghan kingdoms continued to push back. These tensions left Afghanistan open to attack by the Hephthalites.

The Hephthalites, a confederation of Turkic and Indo-European-speaking peoples, held immense power between the fourth and sixth centuries CE, conquering central Asia and parts of India and China. After conquering Afghanistan, they established a stronghold in the Hindu Kush and spread across the Bamiyan Valley. There, they adopted some of the Bactrian Buddhist beliefs. During this

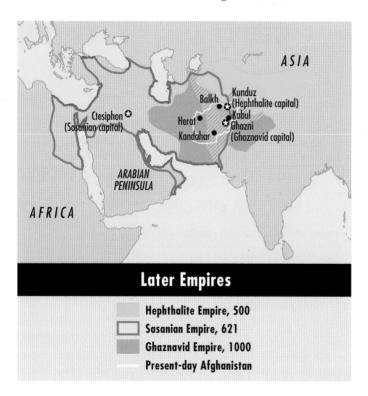

Later Empires

  Hephthalite Empire, 500
  Sasanian Empire, 621
  Ghaznavid Empire, 1000
  Present-day Afghanistan

period, two massive Buddhas were carved into sandstone cliffs. The Hephthalites were harsh rulers, however, and executed scholars, soldiers, artists, musicians, and holy men. They destroyed buildings, artworks, and monasteries.

Enter Islam

In the seventh century, a prophet named Muhammad preached a new religion called Islam. The religion first took hold on the Arabian Peninsula and expanded across to Persia and North Africa. In 642, Arab armies began spreading their religion in the direction of Afghanistan. Afghans resisted at first, but eventually the Muslim armies overtook Balkh and Herat, Afghanistan's most cultural and influential cities. By the early eighth century, nearly all of Afghanistan lived under Muslim leaders. The greatest of those was Mahmud of Ghazni. Mahmud was a great admirer of art and culture, and the city of Ghazni became a religious and cultural center.

Balkh was a thriving city until it was destroyed by the Mongol army in the 1200s. Some evidence of the ancient city remains, including the ruins of a grand mosque built in the 800s.

Mongol Rule

By the thirteenth century, the Mongol Empire had become the largest land empire in history, stretching all the way from Asia's Pacific coast to eastern Europe. The Mongols originally came from a region north of the Gobi Desert in China. They were nomadic herders and fierce, skilled horsemen. Their leader, Genghis Khan, had amassed an enormous and efficient army. He began his invasion of Afghanistan in 1219 and went on to conquer the prosperous cities of Balkh, Ghazni, and Herat, killing hundreds of thousands of people. The Mongol fighters destroyed buildings, irrigation systems, crops, and pasturelands.

After the Mongol Empire weakened, another Mongolian leader, Timur, invaded Afghanistan. He arrived as a military conqueror, but once his rule was established, he revived the Silk Road, and once-prosperous Afghan cities regained some of their former glory. His son, an admirer of art and architecture, rebuilt the city of Herat.

Native Sons

Babur was a descendant of Timur. After generations of heirs had divided up Timur's empire, Babur inherited a small kingdom but was unable to hold on to it. Determined to rule, Babur formed an army and captured Kabul, Kandahar, and ultimately India, where he established his capital. His realm was called the Moghul Empire. Babur was highly educated and a supporter of the arts. He composed an autobiography that described his life as a Muslim as well as everyday life in Afghanistan. His writing provides a valuable historical record of the region's art, architecture, painting, and poetry.

Babur's Moghul Empire ruled southern and eastern Afghanistan while a Persian dynasty, called the Safavid Empire, ruled in the west. In 1722, Afghans revolted and conquered the Safavids. Their leader, Nadir Shah, became king of Persia, what is now called Iran. He then turned his sights on the Moghuls and took over Kandahar and Herat, before invading India to attack the seat of Moghul power. Nadir Shah was cruel to his own people and was murdered by his guards in 1747.

After the assassination, a council of elders held a formal meeting called a *loya jirga* and unanimously chose Ahmad Shah

Dost Muhammad served as king of Afghanistan for more than three decades.

Durrani, an important tribal leader, to become the ruler. It was his mission to get rid of foreign control. He took back Kabul, Ghazni, Kandahar, Herat, and unified many small kingdoms. He wrested land from the Moghuls and became the most powerful Muslim ruler in the world at the time. Ahmad Shah Durrani is considered the founder of modern Afghanistan.

After his death, his many sons feuded, leaving an opening for others to take control of Afghanistan. Foreign powers returned, and the country was once again divided. In 1826, a new ruler named Dost Muhammad took control.

The Great Game

In the early nineteenth century, the Russian Empire and the British Empire engaged in an aggressive rivalry. Russia expanded across central Asia, while Britain had a colonial hold on India and other parts of South Asia. Between the two empires lay the "buffer states," Tibet, Persia, and Afghanistan. Britain was ferociously protective of its most valuable colonies and was fearful that Russia was targeting them. Russia, in the meantime, was steadily expanding across central Asia. Although it was Russia and Britain who were enemies, they played out their battles on Afghan soil. Their posturing came to be known as the Great Game.

When a Russian envoy visited Dost Muhammad in Kabul, British officials worried Russia was advancing. They sought the aid of a leader of the Punjab Empire in India and decided to invade Kabul. With the help of hundreds of war elephants and more than 250 camels carrying supplies, British troops led an invasion over a steep mountain pass. The march itself was exhausting, but the British were successful in the battle. The Afghan army was unable to defend itself against British weapons, and Dost Muhammad was taken hostage.

Dost Muhammad's son Akbar formed an army in the north and rallied rival Afghan groups to join. They marched into Kabul and secured the release of Dost Muhammad. The Afghans forced the British army to abandon their weapons and stockpiles of gold and depart. It was bitter cold and snowing when the British soldiers made their retreat. Many failed to reach India. Some froze or starved, and others were

British troops make their way through the mountains into Afghanistan in 1842.

ambushed. The British realized they should not underestimate the people of Afghanistan.

In 1878, the Russian government sent diplomats to Kabul. The British government demanded that the Afghans allow a British diplomatic mission as well. The Afghans refused, and Britain responded by sending forty thousand troops over the border. The British fared no better in this war in Afghanistan than they had in the first, and by 1881 they were forced to leave. The new Afghan ruler, Abdur Rahman Khan, met with the British and they agreed he would rule Afghanistan, but the British would oversee Afghanistan's foreign relations. By 1907, Russia and Britain had come to terms over their interests in Afghanistan.

Yet in 1917, all treaties were voided. A communist revolution had overthrown the Russian government. Soon, Russia and the Eastern European and Central Asian states it controlled became known as the Soviet Union.

The Durand Line

On November 12, 1893, Afghan ruler Abdur Rahman Khan and a British official, Sir Mortimer Durand, signed an agreement establishing the Afghan/Indian border. Called the Durand Line, the border runs 1,640 miles (2,640 km). In 1947, Pakistan separated from India, so this is today the border between Afghanistan and Pakistan.

From its beginning, the Durand Line has been a source of bitterness and controversy. The border follows natural geography, such as rivers, valleys, and mountain passes, yet it slices through ethnic tribal land. The largest ethnic group in the world is the Pashtuns, whose land is now divided by an international border. More than half the Pashtuns live on the Pakistan side of the border.

The Great Game, Continued

Abdur Rahman Khan's son Habibullah Khan became the leader of Afghanistan upon his father's death in 1901. He brought modernization in the form of electricity and automobiles to Afghanistan. When Habibullah's son Amanullah took the throne in 1919, he declared full Afghan independence and Britain and Afghanistan went to war once again. After a few months, the two nations signed a peace treaty, granting Afghanistan control of its own foreign affairs.

With his newfound authority, Amanullah signed a friendship treaty with the Soviet Union. The Soviets provided Afghanistan with money, technology, and weapons. Amanullah was a forward-thinking man who proposed many reforms. He used Soviet money and technology to build roads and communication networks. He wrote a new constitution granting equal rights to women, and established formal schools for boys and girls. But many of his new policies upset traditional religious leaders. Conservative Afghans were against most of his reforms, and in 1929, Amanullah left the throne.

Amanullah Khan took the throne at age twenty-seven and ruled for a decade. He wanted to modernize the country, but he was not successful because he had poor advisers and inadequate support.

Amanullah's successor, Muhammad Nadir Shah, aligned himself with conservative religious and tribal leaders, and a new constitution was written that gave Afghans fewer rights. Still, he left some of Amanullah's reforms in place. He improved roads, established Kabul University, and created a national banking system.

In 1933, Muhammad Nadir Shah was assassinated, and his nineteen-year-old son, Mohammed Zahir, became the Afghan ruler. His forty-year reign was a rare one of peace. During his reign, he gave women additional rights and established greater religious and political tolerance. In 1973, when Zahir

Queen Soraya

Queen Soraya Tarzi, wife of Amanullah Khan, was a member of a liberal and highly educated family. She encouraged women to "lift the veil," or cease wearing robes and veils to cover themselves in public. She herself stopped wearing a veil, an action viewed as a symbol for the cause of women's rights. Queen Soraya also promoted education for girls. In 1926, the queen said in a speech, "Independence belongs to all of us and that is why we celebrate it. Do you think, however, that our nation from the outset needs only men to serve it? We must all contribute toward the development of our nation and this cannot be done without being equipped with knowledge."

Shah traveled to Italy for medical treatment, his former prime minister, Mohammad Daud Khan, staged a successful coup. Mohammed Zahir Shah was the last Afghan king.

Changing Times

Daud Khan declared himself president and renamed the country the Republic of Afghanistan. He continued modernizing the nation, expanding women's rights and public education. He also promoted the idea of creating a Pashtun state to reunite Pashtuns on both sides of the border.

Daud Khan was initially pro-Soviet, but later he felt his country relied too much on Soviet aid. He expanded and modernized the army and sought aid from other countries, such as Egypt, Iran, India, and Saudi Arabia. He developed new diplomatic relations with the West, including the United

Soviet tanks roll through Afghanistan in 1988. More than a half million Afghans were killed in the decade-long Soviet-Afghan War.

States. These developments angered the Soviets, who feared that Afghanistan would grow too close to the West. In 1978, Daud Khan was assassinated.

The Afghan communist party took over the government. Many Muslim leaders resisted, because the communists opposed religion. The government imprisoned thousands of Muslim leaders. Soviet leaders feared Afghanistan was headed for a civil war. In December 1979, they sent paratroopers into Kabul to prop up Afghanistan's communist government. Muslim leaders and many of their followers fled into the mountains.

An Uneven Fight

The Soviet army took command of the Afghan army. In the mountains, meanwhile, rebel Muslim leaders formed groups known as the *mujahideen*—the term for soldiers who fight in the name of god for Islam. The Soviets, whose military out-

The Lion of Panjshir

Ahmad Shah Massoud was an engineering student in Kabul in the 1970s. He opposed the communist regime and the Soviets' support of it. When the Soviets invaded Afghanistan, Massoud immediately called for action. An ethnic Tajik, he convinced rival tribes to join him in defense of their homeland. He developed strategies for guerrilla warfare against the Soviets, blocking mountain passes and ambushing supply lines. His resourcefulness helped his small army capture weapons, tanks, and even an airfield. His heroism earned him the nickname the Lion of Panjshir (Panjshir being his home province). Once the Soviets withdrew and a new government was formed, Massoud was appointed minister of defense. But the new government fell into chaos as rivals and warlords waged war. Massoud tried to make peace and suggested democratic elections, to no avail. When a rebel group, the Taliban, came to power, Massoud tried again to negotiate peace and call for free elections. Again, he was denied. The Taliban wanted to be rid of Massoud—he was the only leader of the Northern Alliance who had not fled the country. Massoud's popularity stood in their way. On September 9, 2001, two suicide bombers disguised as television reporters came to interview him. Their cameras exploded and Massoud was killed. Three years later, then president Hamid Karzai honored him with the title, "Hero of the Afghan Nation."

numbered the mujahideen by tens of thousands, moved in with tanks and heavy artillery. But the tanks were useless for fighting in the mountains. The Soviets used poison gas and helicopters, but the mujahideen, although armed with old rifles, successfully blockaded mountain passes and laid siege to Kabul. By 1982, the mujahideen controlled three-quarters of the country. The Soviets withdrew in 1989 leaving homes and farms destroyed and five million people homeless. A mujahideen group called the Northern Alliance took over the government of Afghanistan.

The Taliban and the Northern Alliance

The mujahideen were people of many different ethnic groups, including Tajiks, Pashtuns, Hazaras, and Uzbeks. After the Soviet withdrawal, their rivalries returned, and they fought for political power. Afghans had hoped for peace, and instead many were caught up in ethnic fighting.

In the early 1990s, a former mujahid named Mullah Mohammad Omar began condemning the ethnic fighting throughout Afghanistan. Under his guidance, Pashtun students from madrassas (Islamic schools) formed small bands of fighters called the Taliban (*talib* means "religious student"). The Taliban moved from village to village, taking control of local governments. Mullah Omar urged the Taliban to place the villages under strict Islamic, or Sharia, law. At first, nearly every village welcomed the Taliban and their promise of peace. Yet they were unprepared for the Taliban's harsh rules and behavior.

Taliban Rule

The rule of Mullah Omar and the Taliban was severe and unbending. Men were ordered to wear traditional garb—a turban and a loose pantsuit called a *shalwar kamiz*. They were not allowed to shave their beards. Girls and women were required to cover themselves in a *burka*—a full-body robe with a veil that covers the head and face. Girls were not allowed to attend school. Women could not work outside the home and were not to appear in public unless accompanied by a close male relative. The Taliban forbade music, radio, television, and movies. Disobedience was treated with harsh punishment. Villagers who did not agree with the Taliban feared daily for their lives. Many professional people and city dwellers, used to a more liberal lifestyle, fled the country.

As the Taliban grew powerful, the Northern Alliance, under the leadership of Ahmad Shah Massoud, reunited to oppose them. After the Taliban captured Kandahar, they spread into the countryside, destroying villages and imposing Sharia law. In September 1996, Taliban soldiers assassinated Afghan president Mohammad Najibullah Ahmadzai and took control of Kabul. The Northern Alliance retreated to the mountains.

World Stage

In late 1998, the United States was searching for Osama bin Laden, the leader of an Islamic terrorist organization called al-Qaeda. Several al-Qaeda groups lived in the southern hills of Afghanistan, and the Taliban allowed bin Laden to hide among them.

On September 11, 2001, members of al-Qaeda hijacked four planes. They flew two of the planes into the Twin Towers of the World Trade Center in New York City, destroying the buildings. A third jet crashed into the Pentagon, the headquarters of the U.S. military in Virginia, and the fourth into a field in Pennsylvania. Because several of the hijackers had trained in Afghanistan, the United States and its allies invaded the country. The Northern Alliance, enraged by the assassination of Ahmad Shah Massoud, joined the battle. Within two months, the Taliban government toppled. But both bin Laden and Taliban leader Mullah Omar escaped. In November 2001, the Northern Alliance returned to Kabul. A loya jirga chose an acting president, Hamid Karzai.

Out of the Ashes

In 2004, Afghanistan held democratic elections and Karzai, a moderate member of the Pashtun ethnic group, won a five-year term as president. The next year, voting was held for parliament, the first election in thirty years. Many women were elected. In 2009, Karzai won a second term.

Both Mullah Omar and Osama bin Laden have been killed, yet peace has not come to Afghanistan. The Taliban continues to terrorize, and the United States and its allies continue to send more troops and supplies. The constant violence has forced more than one million Afghans to flee their villages and seek refuge in other countries.

The presidential election in 2014 was close. The two leading candidates, Ashraf Ghani, a former finance minister, and

Abdullah Abdullah, a former foreign minister, both declared victory. Under pressure from the United States to settle the election peacefully, the two agreed to share power and form a unity government. Ghani became president and Abdullah was named chief executive, a new position in government. It was Afghanistan's first peaceful transfer of power since 1901.

Although the two leaders have different ideas, they are working on new social and economic programs and countless reconstruction projects. Yet they still contend with bombings, instability, and poverty. After decades of war, Afghans are trying to create a better and more stable country. In many parts of Afghanistan, Afghans are building new schools, hospitals, and roads; setting up stronger local governments; starting new businesses; and improving women's rights.

Students attend school in a tent near Jalalabad. Afghanistan is building many new schools because many more young people are attending school than did so in the past.

CHAPTER 5

Government for the People

FROM THE EARLIEST RECORDED TIMES, AFGHANISTAN has been controlled by, or under attack from, foreign governments. In addition to the mayhem inflicted by outsiders, the country has been plagued by civil wars and ethnic fighting. To this day, Afghanistan's governments have rarely been stable, and as power has changed hands from one ruler to the next, the transition has often been violent. Afghanistan's leaders today face extraordinary challenges, but the people who work in government and the voters who have elected them are working hard to make much-needed changes.

Opposite: **Newly elected members of the Afghan parliament are sworn in.**

The Flag of Afghanistan

No other country has changed its flag as often in one hundred years as Afghanistan has. Today, the Afghan flag is made up of three equal vertical bands. The black band represents foreign occupations of the past, the red band symbolizes the blood of freedom fighters, and the green band symbolizes both agriculture and Islam. The national emblem is in the center of the flag. The emblem consists of a mosque and a pulpit with flags on each side. Circling the emblem are sheaves of wheat and two inscriptions. Above are the words, *La ilaha illa Allah wa-Muhammad rasul Allah*, which means "There is no god but God, and Muhammad is the prophet of God." Below this are rays of sun and the word *Takbir*, meaning "God is great." Below the emblem is the word

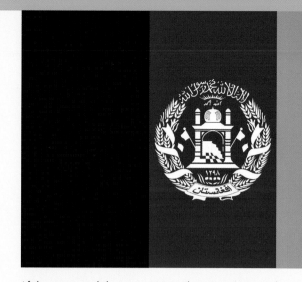

Afghanistan and the year 1298. The year 1298 in the Islamic calendar is the same as the year 1919 in the Western calendar. This is the year Britain recognized Afghanistan's independence.

The Constitution

Afghanistan's constitution has changed frequently throughout its history. The most recent one was approved in 2004. At this time, the country was renamed the Islamic Republic of Afghanistan. Although the constitution declares that Islam is the state religion, it also protects the rights of non-Muslims to practice their religions. The constitution establishes three branches of government—executive, legislative, judicial.

The Executive Branch

The president is the powerful head of the executive branch. He or she serves as the head of state and commander of the Afghan military. The president is elected by secret ballot and must receive more than 50 percent of the vote. If there is no

A Look at the Capital

Kabul, the capital of Afghanistan, is by far the country's largest city. About 3.6 million people live in the city, which is nearly one-tenth of the country's population. Afghans from throughout the country have fled to Kabul in recent decades hoping to escape war and poverty. It is the most ethnically diverse city in Afghanistan. Kabul is an ancient city founded more than 3,500 years ago, but sadly, battles and bombings have destroyed many historic neighborhoods. The presidential palace and other government buildings, such as the National Archives and the foreign embassies, are inside a walled

compound in the heart of the oldest part of the city. Otherwise, new, crowded neighborhoods fan out from the city center and streets are clogged with cars and trucks. Surrounding the city are snow-capped mountains of the Hindu Kush.

Kabul is also the nation's cultural center. There are two major art museums and several universities. The city has many traditional marketplaces and lively alleys filled with vendors' stalls. In recent years, many new restaurants, shopping malls, theaters, and swimming pools have opened across the city. Foreign governments are helping to build new schools and hospitals, as well as transportation and communication services.

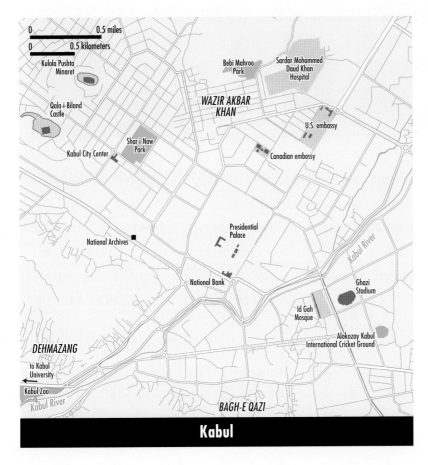

0   0.5 miles
0   0.5 kilometers

Kulola Pushta Minaret
Bebi Mahroo Park
Sardar Mohammed Daud Khan Hospital
Qala-i-Biland Castle
WAZIR AKBAR KHAN
U.S. embassy
Shar-i-Naw Park
Kabul City Center
Canadian embassy
Presidential Palace
National Archives
Kabul River
National Bank
Ghazi Stadium
Id Gah Mosque
Alokozay Kabul International Cricket Ground
DEHMAZANG
to Kabul University
Kabul Zoo
Kabul River
BAGH-E QAZI

Kabul

President Ashraf Ghani (left) and Chief Executive Abdullah Abdullah (right) share leadership of Afghanistan. The position of chief executive was created solely to resolve the disputed election between Ghani and Abdullah.

clear winner, a runoff election is held, and the candidate with the majority votes is elected.

In the 2014 election, there was no clear winner. The best option was to share the top executive position. Ashraf Ghani was chosen as president and Abdullah Abdullah was given the title of chief executive. They formed the National Unity Government (NUG).

Other members of the executive branch include two vice presidents and cabinet ministers. The cabinet ministers are appointed by the president and, in the case of the NUG, the chief executive. The cabinet ministers must be approved by the National Assembly.

The National Anthem

According to the 2004 constitution, the Afghan national anthem must be in the Pashto language, include the names of Afghan ethnic groups, and include the phrase "God is great." A new national anthem was selected in 2006. Its lyrics are by Abdul Bari Jahani and the music is by Babrak Wassa.

English translation

This land is Afghanistan
It is the pride of every Afghan
The land of peace, the land of sword
Its sons are all braves.

This is the country of every tribe
Land of Balochs, and Uzbeks
Pashtuns, and Hazaras
Turkmen and Tajiks.

With them, Arabs and Gojars
Pamirian, Nuristanian

Barahawi, and Qizilbash
Also Aimaq, and Pashai.

This land will shine forever
Like the sun in the blue sky
In the chest of Asia
It will remain as heart forever.

We will follow the one God.
We all say, God is great,
We all say, God is great,
We all say, God is great.

An Afghan voter displays a finger stained with ink. When Afghans vote, a finger is dipped in ink to show that they have already voted and cannot vote again.

The Legislative Branch

Afghanistan's National Assembly is the lawmaking, or legislative, branch of the government. The National Assembly has two houses. The lower house is called the House of the People, and the upper house is called the House of Elders. The members of the House of the People are elected by direct vote of the people. Two-thirds of the members of the House of Elders are chosen by district councils. The final third is appointed by the president and chief executive. The president and the chief executive appoint well-known experts and scholars. These appointments are required to be inclusive. Fifty percent must be women, at least two people must have a disability, and two people must belong to the Kuchi ethnic group, a nomadic tribe without a permanent settlement.

The Favored Daughter

In 2014, Fawzia Koofi, the head of a political party called Movement for Change in Afghanistan, announced she would run for president. She declared, "We must come out of the days of darkness, and bring about change." Koofi was aware that traditionalists would not vote for her, but she wanted to inspire young people, especially young women. She had already made her mark in history by being the first woman deputy speaker of the National Assembly.

Koofi is recognized around the world for her fighting spirit in speaking out for women's rights, education for girls, employment opportunities for women, and women's health care. She presented a bill to the National Assembly called the Elimination of Violence Against Women. While conservative members of the assembly blocked the law, all thirty-four provinces adopted the law for their court systems.

Though Koofi came from a somewhat privileged background—her father was a member of the National Assembly—she knows only too well the challenges of being a woman in Afghanistan. Her father had seven wives and twenty-three children and did not believe in educating his daughters. On her own, she became the first woman in her family to go to school. She has been threatened many times by the Taliban but accepts the risk. In her book *The Favored Daughter* she wrote, "Perhaps someday your children's children will grow up free in a proud, successful, Islamic republic that has taken its rightful place in the developed world."

In many villages, the community participates in local law-making. In a meeting called a *shura*, people gather to study the issues and listen to each other's suggestions and opinions. Once a decision is made, everyone must accept the new law or plan. In 2017, for example, the president promised thousands of villages money to help them improve their communities. Each village called a shura to decide how to spend the money. Some chose to help build a school, dig a community well, or join other villages in funding a regional health clinic.

The Presidential Palace

Afghanistan's National Government

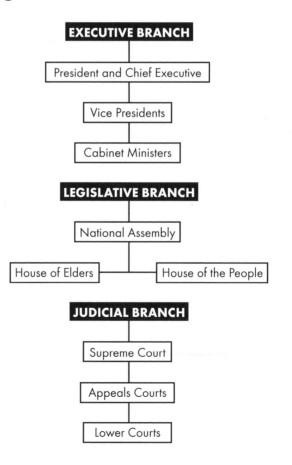

EXECUTIVE BRANCH

President and Chief Executive

Vice Presidents

Cabinet Ministers

LEGISLATIVE BRANCH

National Assembly

House of Elders | House of the People

JUDICIAL BRANCH

Supreme Court

Appeals Courts

Lower Courts

A *jirga* is a centuries-old Afghan decision-making council. It is made up of local leaders and tribal elders. Each district or province may convene a jirga to discuss community needs and concerns, such as whether to build a well or repair a road. A jirga is not legally binding, but as a traditional form of government, essentially everyone accepts the council's decision.

On a national level, Afghanistan has a *loya jirga*, meaning grand council. There are 398 districts and 34 provinces in Afghanistan. Each district chooses someone to represent them. This could be a tribal elder, a religious figure, or a political leader. A loya jirga requires that a certain number of seats are reserved for women, refugees, nomads, and general citizens. All ethnic, religious, and tribal groups must be represented. A loya jirga is called only for reasons of major national importance. In the past, they have been called upon to declare war, choose a ruler, make social reforms, or approve a constitution. The loya jirga's decision is not final until approved

by both houses of the National Assembly, as well as the president and the chief executive.

Loya jirgas have been involved in selecting Ahmad Shah to be king, selecting Hamid Karzai to be acting president after the fall of the Taliban in 2002, and approving the new constitution in 2004.

The Judicial Branch

The head of the judicial branch is the Supreme Court. The nine members, including one chief justice, are appointed by the president for a ten-year term. The appointments must be approved by the House of the People. Beneath the Supreme Court are the Appeals Courts, which hear cases that have already been tried in lower courts. Lower courts are made up of district, municipal, and village courts.

CHAPTER 6

Making a Living

N RECENT DECADES, AFGHANS HAVE LIVED WITH WAR, and for centuries, most have lived in poverty. Yet, today, the country's economy is starting to grow, especially in the cities. With the help of government programs, foreign aid, and new businesses, the economy is also improving in rural areas. Afghanistan hopes new technologies and new ideas will help create jobs and improve people's lives.

Opposite: **An Afghan farmer harvests wheat, Afghanistan's largest crop.**

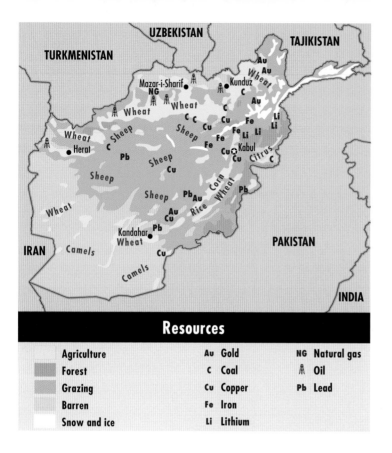

Map labels:
UZBEKISTAN
TURKMENISTAN
TAJIKISTAN
Mazar-i-Sharif
NG
Wheat
Kunduz
C
Au
Au
Wheat
Wheat
C
C
Cu
Cu
Fe
Li
Herat
Wheat
Sheep
Sheep
Fe
Li
Li
Fe
Cu
Kabul
C
Pb
Cu
Citrus
C
Sheep
Cu
Sheep
Pb
Au
Corn
Pb
Au
Rice
Wheat
Wheat
Cu
Kandahar
Pb
Wheat
Cu
Camels
IRAN
Camels
PAKISTAN
INDIA

Resources

▦ Agriculture	Au Gold	NG Natural gas
▦ Forest	C Coal	⚒ Oil
▦ Grazing	Cu Copper	Pb Lead
▦ Barren	Fe Iron	
▦ Snow and ice	Li Lithium	

Agriculture

More than three-quarters of Afghans depend on farming and raising livestock to make a living. Yet less than 15 percent of the land is suitable for farming. In some provinces, larger commercial farms grow crops to sell in local markets, city markets, and for export to other countries.

In the east, farmers grow fruits, such as apples, apricots, grapes, and mulberries. There are also orchards of walnuts, almonds, and pistachios. The eastern provinces of Nuristan and Laghman have large wheat farms. Wheat and rice are the most important staple crops. Rice is grown throughout the northeastern provinces. In the north, crops include melons, vegetables, wheat, alfalfa, and seed oil crops, such as sunflower and sesame. Western areas around Herat are known for grapes, pistachios, and spices, including saffron. Saffron comes from the crocus flower, which is native to Afghanistan. Workers must harvest as many as seventy-five thousand flowers to produce a single pound (0.5 kilograms) of saffron. Considered the world's most expensive spice, saffron can cost as much as $5,000 per pound.

In the south, farmers produce crops such as pomegranates, walnuts, and apricots. Large farms grow feed for livestock,

including wheat, corn, alfalfa, and clover. Nearly two-thirds of all crops grown in Afghanistan require irrigation. Water is taken from rivers and underground wells and springs and is channeled into open ditches and tunnels.

Women harvest saffron crocuses near Herat.

Fantastic Fur

Several decades ago, Afghanistan produced many crops for export. But years of war damaged growing regions, and many farmers abandoned their farms. Today, farmers are again selling products to other countries.

Cashmere is a relatively new export product for Afghanistan. Cashmere is the winter layer of soft, fluffy hair that grows underneath the fur of a goat. Nearly all the goats in Afghanistan produce cashmere. Traditionally, Afghans collected the undercoat and burned it to heat their homes. The herders raised goats for hides and food, not hair. Now, though, several foreign companies are investing in Afghan cashmere production, and the nation's more than 450,000 goat herders realize there is money to be made from selling cashmere. There are new processing plants where workers comb, clean, refine, and spin the cashmere into yarn. Today, Afghanistan is the third-largest producer of luxury cashmere in the world.

What Afghanistan Grows, Makes, and Mines

AGRICULTURE (2015)

Wheat	5,370,259 metric tons
Grapes	744,847 metric tons
Sheep	13,500,000 animals

MANUFACTURING (Statistics unavailable)

Food processing
Textiles
Construction materials

MINING

Natural gas (2014)	159,600,000 cubic meters
Coal (2012)	1,240,000 metric tons
Salt (2013)	145,000 metric tons

Livestock

People raise livestock in several regions around Afghanistan. The steppe grasslands are prime pasture for sheep and goats. Afghanistan is noted for raising Karakul sheep. Its wool is used in carpet making and its lambskin is highly prized. Cattle are also raised in the northern regions for meat and dairy products. In the Wakhan Corridor, Wakhi and Kyrgyz herders raise yaks and camels. Both types of animals are used for transporting heavy loads and for riding. They also supply milk, meat, and fur. Most rural families raise chickens for meat and eggs. Many Afghan women raise bees to make honey.

South of Kabul lies a 375-mile (600-km) vein of copper called the Afghan Copper Belt. Home to three enormous copper deposits, the area has lured a Chinese mining company to invest in building a large-scale mine. The value of the agreement is a vital step toward Afghanistan's economic recovery.

However, there is a problem. At the mine's site is an ancient buried Buddhist city, called Mes Aynak, along the route of the Silk Road. Archaeologists working there have recently discovered a treasure trove of Buddhist artifacts from the reign of Alexander the Great. They have unearthed statues, altars, carvings, pottery, gold coins, and jewelry.

Archaeologists say that they will need at least twenty-five years to properly excavate the priceless relics. The mining company and the Afghanistan government cannot wait that long. It is believed the site will produce $40 billion worth of copper. Caught in a dilemma, an Afghan government mining official

said, "From one side, my people need food. We are poor people. My national budget needs to generate revenue. But on the other side, I have to protect the international heritage."

Mining

Afghanistan has some of the earliest records of mining anywhere in the world, dating back more than six thousand years. Today, vast mineral deposits lie beneath the ground in the country. Geologists and mining experts estimate that at least one trillion dollars' worth of minerals could be mined in Afghanistan. Besides metals such as copper, iron, gold, platinum, and silver, there are minerals vital to modern technology, such as lithium, which is used to make batteries for computers and smartphones. Afghanistan's mineral wealth

also includes gems such as emeralds, rubies, amethysts, and topaz. Afghanistan is the world's leading producer of the brilliant blue gemstone called lapis lazuli. Talc, salt, zinc, sulfur, chromite, marble, coal, oil, and natural gas are also removed from the ground in Afghanistan.

Manufacturing

Manufacturing has never been a large part of the Afghan economy. Historically, products were often handmade. Skills were handed down from parent to child, and villages and provinces were often known for making specialized items, such as leather saddles or shoes, woven rugs, pottery, or glass.

Coins and Banknotes

The basic unit of Afghan currency is the afghani, which is divided into 100 puls. Coins come in values of 1, 2, and 5 afghanis. Banknotes come in values of 1, 2, 5, 10, 20, 50, 100, 500, and 1,000 afghanis.

In 2014, Afghanistan issued new banknotes, which have magnetic stripes and holograms to make it easier to identify fake banknotes. The notes have significant scenes from Afghan culture. The 500 afghani banknote shows both ancient and modern elements. The Great Mosque of Herat is on the front and the Kandahar airport tower is on the reverse. In 2017, 67 afghanis equaled US$1.

Today, most factories are located in cities. In Kabul and Mazar-i-Sharif, workers produce cotton textiles, wool, felt, and cashmere yarn. There are also many shoe and furniture factories. New chemical plants are producing fertilizers and medicines.

Food processing is the largest manufacturing industry in the country. In small factories, workers dry and roast nuts, fruits, and coffee beans; butcher and cure meat; and make cheese, yogurt, and butter. There are also flour mills and factories that press sunflower and sesame seeds into cooking oils.

Years of war have destroyed roads, buildings, and machinery. Slowly, factories are gearing up to manufacture or make replacement parts for farm and construction equipment, such as tractors, plows, road graders, and backhoes. Around the country, sawmills cut lumber and factories churn out bricks and cement to serve the robust construction industry.

Services

In Afghanistan, the service industry employs about 15 percent of the workforce, yet contributes more than half of the nation's gross domestic product (GDP), the total value of all the goods and services produced in the country. Service workers include teachers, doctors, bus drivers, government workers, military personnel, construction workers, sanitation workers, hotel and restaurant employees, shopkeepers, and bankers.

Workers lay plastic pipes at a construction site in Kunduz. After years of war, construction in Afghanistan has revived in recent times.

Energy

Energy is key to Afghanistan's progress, and the country's people need to be supplied with reliable electricity. One hurdle in obtaining this is that the nation has countless miles of power lines to install. Currently, only about half of households in Afghanistan have electricity. In cities it is frequently unreliable, and in rural areas, when the sun sets, people rely on candles and oil lamps. Without electricity, factories, workshops, and schools shut down after dark. There is no refrigeration. Cell phones and laptops cannot be charged. When electricity comes to a village, schools improve, health clinics offer better services, and factories and workshops can modernize and become more efficient. In 2009, when Kabul became the first Afghan city to offer twenty-four-hour electric power, its economy improved.

Afghanistan imports more than three-quarters of its electricity. About 20 percent of its home-grown energy comes from hydropower dams along rivers. It has plans to improve the output of hydroelectric power and to use more of its own oil and natural gas. Renewable energy sources are also growing in importance. The first wind-generated power plant was built in the Panjshir Valley and supplies electricity to government buildings. In Bamiyan Province, a massive solar energy plant provides electricity for 2,500 households. Kandahar, which is sunny almost year-round, has become a hub for solar energy, and Kandahar University has established a solar energy department.

CHAPTER 7

Many Voices

FOR CENTURIES, AFGHANISTAN WAS A BUSY CROSSROADS for trade between continents. It also withstood many invasions. This mixture of travelers, soldiers, nomads, and immigrants settled in the area and eventually formed a nation. The settlers had little in common. Different ethnic groups kept to themselves, living in villages governed by local leaders. These groups are made up of smaller groups, or tribes, and are divided further still into extended family groups, or clans.

Opposite: **An Afghan father and son. Afghanistan has one of the youngest populations in the world. About 41 percent of Afghans are under the age of fifteen and just 6.5 percent are over age fifty-four.**

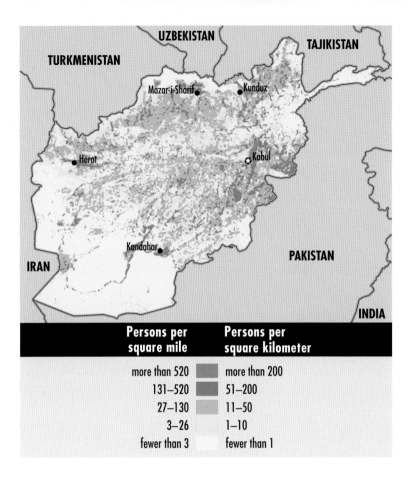

Persons per square mile	Persons per square kilometer
more than 520	more than 200
131–520	51–200
27–130	11–50
3–26	1–10
fewer than 3	fewer than 1

The constitution of 2004 specifically mentions fourteen ethnic groups—Pashtun, Tajik, Hazara, Uzbek, Baloch, Turkmen, Nuristani, Pamiri, Arab, Gujar, Brahui, Qizilbash, Aimaq, and Pashai. Afghanistan is also home to smaller ethnic groups, such as the Wakhi and Kyrgyz. More than thirty-three million people call Afghanistan home, and most ethnic groups carefully preserve their own ethnic identities.

The Way of the Pashtun

The Pashtun ethnic group is the largest in Afghanistan, making up about 42 percent of the population. Pashtuns are Sunni Muslims and their traditional homeland is south of the Hindu Kush. There are several Pashtun tribes. The two most influential tribes are the Durrani and the Ghilzai. Traditionally, people belonging to the Durrani tribe have held leadership positions. Many are city dwellers and businesspeople. The Ghilzai people are traditionally herders and farmers, and many become soldiers. Although Durrani Pashtuns have long held political power, President Ashraf Ghani and many cabinet ministers and advisers are members of the Ghilzai tribe.

The Pashtun people follow an ancient code of conduct called Pashtunwali, or "the way of the Pashtun." First and foremost, they are loyal and strongly independent. The Pashtun people are very hospitable, as are all Afghans. Guests are treated with generosity and honor, and are welcomed even if they belong to a traditionally hostile tribe. Another time-honored belief is a duty to avenge family or tribe against any crime or insult. Some disputes can end up as feuds that go on for generations. Bravery, respect for others, and righteousness are other important beliefs. Followers of Pashtunwali defend their land, family, and honor at all costs.

A Tajik woman shows her newborn to her mother-in-law. Women in Afghanistan have an average of five children.

The Tajik People

The Tajik people, who live in the northeast and the west, are the nation's second-largest ethnic group, accounting for about

27 percent of the population. A fair number of Tajik people are well-to-do. Many Tajiks are well-educated city dwellers who work in business, public service, and government. Others follow traditional careers as artisans, farmers, or herders. The Tajik have cultural ties to Tajikistan and Iran. Ahmad Shah Massoud, a leader of the Northern Alliance, was Tajik. Abdullah Abdullah, chief executive of Afghanistan, has a mixed Tajik-Pashtun heritage and mostly identifies with the Tajik ethnic group.

Hazara women attend a protest in 2016. Although no longer persecuted as they were under the Taliban, Hazara people continue to suffer discrimination.

Top Ten

Aziz Royesh, a Hazara teacher in Kabul, was chosen as one of the ten best teachers in the world in 2015. Royesh attended school until only the age of ten, when Soviet tanks overran his village. His family fled to Pakistan where he studied on his own. He opened his first school for Afghan refugees in Pakistan and later opened a school in Kabul.

After decades of war, Royesh had to start his school in Kabul from scratch. He made frequent trips across the border to Pakistan, risking his life to buy school supplies. He is tremendously proud to be honored as one of the world's ten best teachers, but he is prouder that nearly half of his students are girls and that many go on to higher education.

Set Apart

The third-largest group in Afghanistan is the Hazaras, who make up approximately 20 percent of the population. For centuries, they have suffered from prejudice and injustice. Unlike most Afghans, Hazaras are Shi'a Muslims. Their facial features are more Asian in appearance than other Afghans.

In the 1890s, the Hazara suffered religious persecution and were enslaved and sold. In addition, many were murdered during the rule of Abdur Rahman Khan. Their homelands near the Helmand River were taken away and given to the Pashtun Kuchi tribe. The Taliban, too, have mercilessly targeted the Hazara people. The Hazara people are now spread widely across Afghanistan. Many young people are moving to Kabul, Herat, and Mazar-i-Sharif to attend school and look for better-paying jobs.

Not until the Afghan constitution of 2004 were the Hazara people granted equal rights. Hazara women have more freedom than women in other ethnic groups. They attend school in nearly equal numbers as males. The first woman mayor and the first woman governor in Afghanistan were both Hazara.

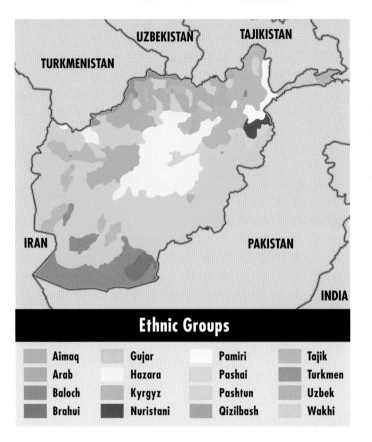

Ethnic Groups

Aimaq	Gujar	Pamiri	Tajik
Arab	Hazara	Pashai	Turkmen
Baloch	Kyrgyz	Pashtun	Uzbek
Brahui	Nuristani	Qizilbash	Wakhi

Turkic People

The Uzbeks, who make up about 10 percent of the population, are Turkic people who migrated to northern Afghanistan from central Asia. Most Uzbek people live in the north, close to the border of Uzbekistan. Uzbek farmers make a good living growing and harvesting grains, vegetables, and cotton. Uzbeks are also successful business owners and skilled artisans. They are particularly known for their superb carpets, traditionally woven by women.

The Afghan Turkmen are descended from a nomadic group that migrated from central Asia and settled between Balkh and Herat. Traditionally herders, the Turkmen introduced the prized Karakul sheep to Afghanistan. They have prospered by selling Karakul coats, hats, and pelts. Like their Uzbek neighbors, they are known for their finely woven carpets.

Population of Major Cities (2013 est.)

Kabul	3,589,000
Kandahar	491,500
Herat	436,300
Mazar-i-Sharif	368,100
Kunduz	304,600

Other Groups

Several smaller ethnic groups are nomadic or seminomadic. Once nomadic, the Aimaq people now farm in regions near Herat. The Baloch people were nomads who came to Afghanistan through Iran and settled in the southern provinces. The Kuchi are nomadic people belonging to the Pashtun tribe.

They move across the Helmand River valley herding sheep, goats, donkeys, and camels. They barter meat, milk, cheese, and wool to farmers for grains, fruits, and vegetables. The population of Kuchi nomads has shrunk over decades of war, because many of their grazing lands have become battlefields. Some have given up their nomadic life and moved near cities.

In the remote Wakhan Corridor, the nomadic Kyrgyz are nearly always moving, herding goats, camels, and yaks. They travel with portable homes, dome-shaped tents called yurts, which are covered in animal skins and lined with felted wool rugs. Their Kyrgyz ancestors settled in the region in the fifteenth century and their lifestyle and language have barely changed.

Kyrgyz people gather water from a stream in the Wakhan Corridor.

The Wakhi people came to the Pamir Mountains as refugees in the nineteenth and twentieth centuries. The Wakhi are farmers who plant crops in the spring and move to higher ground to graze their sheep, goats, and yaks in summer. Winter is a difficult time because of the cold. Most Wakhi children do not attend school regularly.

The Qizilbash people belong to a Shi'a sect. Most live in cities. They are generally well educated and have professional careers.

The Nuristani people are an isolated group. The Nuristan Province is one of narrow valleys and steep hills that deter outsiders from coming near. Within the province, most transportation is by foot. The Nuristani people are likely descended from the earliest Greek invaders. Many have light skin, fair hair, and blue or green eyes. Nuristani women are farmers and the men are herders. Meals are simple, but both men and women must contribute. A woman will bring something from the field or orchard, and a man will bring meat or dairy products to the table. The Nuristani people are Sunni Muslim today, but just a century ago, they practiced a form of Hinduism.

Language

More than forty languages are spoken in Afghanistan. Although there are two official languages, in many places, native languages are more likely to be spoken. In 1936, Zahir Shah wanted to unify the tribes and decreed that Pashto, the language of the Pashtun people, would be the official language. However, only one-third of Afghans spoke Pashto. In

An Afghan girl writes
in Dari in a notebook.
About half of Afghans
speak Dari.

1964, Dari was added as the second official language. Native speakers of Dari include Tajiks, Hazaras, and Aimaqs. Many people speak both Pashto and Dari, as well as their traditional tribal language. Ethnic groups that speak a Turkic language include Uzbek, Turkmen, Baloch, and Nuristani.

The Written Word

The Dari and Pashto languages are written in Arabic script. The Arabic alphabet includes twenty-eight letters. Words are written from right to left. Turkic languages are written in either Cyrillic or Arabic. Cyrillic is an alphabet used in Russia, much of eastern Europe, and north and central Asia.

CHAPTER 8

Devotions

ISLAM IS THE PRIMARY RELIGION IN AFGHANISTAN today, but this was not always so. As foreign traders, invaders, and immigrants passed through Afghanistan, they brought their religions with them. Many of the world's religions made a mark on Afghanistan, including Christianity, Judaism, Hinduism, and Buddhism. Today, just 1 percent of Afghans follow these religions. It is unknown how many Christians live in Afghanistan, and no public places of Christian worship remain. As of 2017, two small Hindu temples still stood in Kabul.

Islam originated in the seventh century in the Arabian Peninsula. Arab Muslims spread the religion to neighboring regions, and by the eleventh century, nearly all of

Opposite: **A Muslim boy prays in Kandahar.**

An old, highly decorated Qur'an from Afghanistan

Afghanistan was converted to Islam. Today, 99 percent of Afghans are Muslim.

The Origins of Islam

Islam began about six hundred years after Christianity and more than three thousand years after Judaism. Each of these religions believe in a single god and believe that god has sent messengers, known as prophets, to deliver his word. Muslims believe there have been many prophets, including Moses, Abraham, and Jesus, but they believe that a man named Muhammad was the final prophet.

Muhammad was born in Mecca, in what is now Saudi Arabia, in 570 CE. Muhammad grew to be a kind and intelligent man. He married and had six children. His sons died young. His daughter, Fatimah, however, married a family cousin named Ali. In what would become a crucial part of Islam, Fatimah and Ali's descendants became the prophet's direct line of succession.

Muhammad often went to the desert to think and pray.

"The world is green and beautiful and God has appointed you his steward over it."

"Beware of envy for envy devours good works like the fire devours fuel."

"The search for knowledge is a sacred duty imposed upon every Muslim. Go in search of knowledge."

"Little, but sufficient, is better than the abundant and the alluring."

One day, it is said, the angel Gabriel came to him, bringing the word of God (*Allah* in Arabic). For twenty-two years, Muhammad returned to the desert to receive guidance and words of faith from God. The words Muhammad recorded became the Islamic holy book, the Qur'an.

Muslims call the Qur'an the word of God. They believe that the Bible is also God's word, but they believe that the Qur'an is God's final word. Another book, the Hadith, is Muhammad's interpretations of God's word. The Hadith includes advice and sayings to guide people to live a moral life.

Practicing the Faith

Afghans practice Islam in different ways. The two major groups are Shi'a and Sunni. This division goes back to the death of Muhammad. After he died, some people believed Muslim leadership should belong to his descendants, beginning with his cousin and son-in-law, Ali. They became known as Shi'a, a shortened version of "followers of Ali." The other sect, called Sunni, believed any devout religious scholars could lead.

Sufism is another form of Islam. Some of the earliest Muslims in Afghanistan were Sufis. They sometimes use music and dance to enter a trance state to experience God. Today,

Sufi men in Kabul. Sufism is a mystical form of Islam, and its followers believe they can have a direct personal experience of God.

there are many Sufi mosques and shrines in Afghanistan.

Muslims worship in a mosque whenever they can, but Shi'a and Sufi Muslims also worship at shrines that honor religious scholars or saints. Sunni Muslims believe that practice is against the teachings of Islam.

Sufi Poet

Khwaja Abdullah Ansari, a Sufi mystic and saint, was born in Herat in 1006. A philosopher, teacher, and Qur'an scholar, he is regarded as one of the finest Sufi poets. Ansari is known for his simple, but moving language, such as is found in the poem "Give Me":

O Lord, give me a heart
I can pour out in thanksgiving.
Give me life
So I can spend it
Working for the salvation of the world.

Ansari died in 1088, and a shrine was built around his tomb just outside of Herat. The elegant shrine complex has long been a pilgrimage site for Muslims.

The Five Pillars of Islam

The five pillars of Islam are religious duties. The first pillar is a simple statement of faith called the *shahadah*: "There is no god but God, and Muhammad is the messenger of God."

The second pillar is *salat*, or prayer. Sunni Muslims pray five times a day and Shi'a Muslims pray three times a day. The call to prayer is often broadcast from the tower, or minaret, of a mosque. Traditionally, a spiritual leader would call Muslims to prayer, but today many calls to prayer are recordings. Muslims can also look up the exact times to pray on the internet or by using a cell phone app. The times to pray occur at dawn, midday, late afternoon, sunset, and between sunset and midnight. Before they pray, Muslims wash their hands, arms, face, ankles, and feet. Prayer begins with a person standing and reciting "*Allahu Akbar*," "God is great." The person continues by reciting lines from the Qur'an and giving thanks while bowing, kneeling, and dropping the forehead to

Religious Holidays

Religious holidays in Afghanistan are generally quiet affairs. People come together to share a meal and visit family and friends. Afghan holy days are based on the Islamic calendar, which is eleven days shorter than the Gregorian, or Western, calendar. Because of this, Muslim holidays fall on different dates in the Western calendar each year.

Ashura	Commemorates the death of Muhammad's grandson, Hossain
Mawlid al-Nabi	Muhammad's birthday
Lailat al Miraj	Commemorates Muhammad's journey to Jerusalem where he was given the instruction for Muslims to pray five times daily
Ramadan	A full month commemorating the first revelation of the Qur'an to Muhammad
Eid al-Fitr	Feast at the end of Ramadan
Eid al-Adha	Honors the willingness of the Prophet Ibrahim (Abraham) to sacrifice the life of his son for God

A man prays on the roof of a building in Kunduz. Since Muslims pray frequently throughout the day, formal prayer occurs in many different places.

Religion in Afghanistan

Sunni Muslim	80%
Shi'a Muslim	19%
Other (Christian, Hindu, Sikh, Buddhist, etc.)	1%

the floor. Since it is disrespectful to pray on a dirty surface, Muslims pray on mats or rugs. Following tradition, only men pray inside a mosque. But many modern Afghan Muslims want equal rights for women. Today, 20 percent of mosques in Kabul have special prayer areas for women.

The third pillar of Islam is fasting, or *sawm*. Muslims believe that fasting reminds them of the less fortunate and brings them closer to God. Muslims often fast throughout the year, but every Muslim, except the young and the frail, fasts during the month of Ramadan, the ninth month of the Islamic calendar. During Ramadan, Muslims go without eating or drinking every day from dawn until sunset.

The fourth pillar of Islam is charity, *zakat*. Muslims take every opportunity to give to the poor and share with those less fortunate.

The fifth pillar of Islam is a pilgrimage to Mecca, the birthplace of Muhammad. The last pillar is not a daily or annual duty, but rather a once in a lifetime duty for Muslims who are fit and financially able to travel. The pilgrimage, called the *hajj*, occurs during the twelfth month of the Islamic calendar and lasts for several days. All hajj pilgrims wear white. Wearing the same white garments shows that the pilgrims are equal; there are no signs of wealth or social status.

Afghan men prepare special treats for Eid al-Fitr, a celebration that takes place at the end of Ramadan.

CHAPTER 9

Inspirations

OVER THE CENTURIES, FROM ANCIENT TIMES TO the present, the many groups that came to Afghanistan each brought their own art, music, and ideas, creating an Afghan culture that is rich and multilayered.

The Silk Road brought rich traditions to Afghanistan's ancient cities and remote valleys. Many valuable artifacts have been discovered. Among them is a two-thousand-year-old sculpture of a Kushan Buddhist emperor. Another two-thousand-year-old discovery is a collection of twenty thousand gold and gemstone jewelry pieces, called the Bactrian Hoard, found buried in the tombs of nomadic tribespeople in northern Afghanistan.

In the sixth century BCE, the Achaemenid Empire combined Greek, Persian, and other Asian styles. The Achaemenids carved sculptures onto walls, crafted elaborate metal jewelry, and decorated objects with colored tiles. They constructed

Opposite: **A two-thousand-year-old gold ram is among the thousands of objects that make up the Bactrian Hoard.**

A fragment of a Buddhist oil wall painting from the Bamiyan Valley. The murals in this area are believed to be the world's first oil paintings.

walled cities and elaborate temples and tombs. A site in southern Afghanistan near Kandahar holds thousands of detailed clay statues dating back more than two thousand years. The sculptures have classic Greek and Roman designs such as swirling vines, wreaths of flowers, and toga-like robes. Some of the sculptures portray the diversity of the population, such as royalty, outsiders, monks, soldiers, and nomadic herders.

Painting

The oldest oil paintings in the world are believed to have been murals painted in the sixth century on cliffs and altars near the massive Buddhas sculpted into the cliffs in the Bamiyan Valley. Paints were crafted from seed oils and plant dyes. The images

The National Museum

The National Museum in Kabul housed one of the most important collections of antiquities in the world. Before the 1990s, the museum held more than 100,000 objects. In 1993, the museum was caught in the crossfire of the civil war. After rocket attacks destroyed much of the collection, looters stepped in and made off with much of what remained. Many items were taken into Pakistan and sold illegally. The government ordered museum staff to catalog and preserve the most valuable of the remaining parts of the collection. The objects were locked in metal boxes and hidden. In March 2001, the Taliban ransacked the museum and smashed any artwork that bore the likeness of a human form or face.

When the Taliban government was toppled, the museum staff revealed where the art was hidden—in the National Bank, the presidential palace, and vaults in Switzerland, Germany, and Great Britain. Many of the broken pieces are being restored.

The staff was overjoyed when they recovered the

gold objects from the Bactrian Hoard that had been hidden in the basement of the presidential palace. That collection was shown in Europe and the United States, helping raise money for the museum's restoration.

showed Buddhas in flowing robes surrounded by lush gardens.

Herat has long been a center of Afghan art and culture. Centuries ago, Herat was particularly known for blending art with poetry. Poems were written using decorative writing called calligraphy. Many were illustrated with small, highly detailed paintings. Kamal ud-Din Behzad was considered the best miniature painter in Herat. He was often called upon to illustrate books and poetry, including copies of the Qur'an. He painted with brilliant natural pigments, ground gemstones, silver, and gold.

Shamsia Hassani works on a graffiti painting in Kabul. She wears a mask so she does not breathe in any of the spray paint she is using.

Since the arrival of Islam, Afghan painting has followed a traditional course. Muslim artists rarely depict humans or animals because God is thought to be the only creator. Some refrain from depicting humans out of their own personal belief, while others fear the reaction of more religious people. In Afghanistan, most artists make abstract shapes and highly detailed geometric and floral patterns.

Modern Art

After the Taliban banned art, music, and most forms of enter-tainment, artists disappeared from the public eye. When the Taliban left, many artists literally took to the streets. There were no galleries left to show off their artwork, so artists started painting on vacant buildings and crumbling walls. Their bold art incorporated social and political themes. In many parts of the world, graffiti is outlaw art, but in Afghanistan, it is respected. One of the most famous graffiti artists is Shamsia Hassani. She has shown her work in galleries in Paris and New York City and is a professor of art at Kabul University.

Architecture

Afghanistan's architectural treasures include Greek temples, Buddhist shrines, Islamic minarets (towers), and Mongol and Macedonian walled citadels. Most Afghan architects believed that the decoration of buildings was as important as the construction. Herat is home to much of the nation's architectural wonders. In Herat, the Mousallah Complex, a group of minarets, a mosque, and a madrassa, are all decorated with blue tile mosaics. The Great Mosque of Herat, also known as the Friday Mosque, is more than eight hundred years old, and is considered one of the finest Islamic buildings in Central Asia. Its tall minarets are encircled with

Colorful, complex tile patterns blanket the Friday Mosque in Herat.

calligraphy and tile mosaics of flowers, swirls, and geometric shapes. As a result of many battles, the mosque has fallen into disrepair. Tiles have dropped off, and bright paint has faded. Artisans assigned to restore the mosque are using new colors and more modern mosaics and calligraphy. The mosque is becoming a blend of ancient and modern architecture.

In Mazar-i-Sharif stands the Shrine of Hazrat Ali, also known as the Blue Mosque. It is one of the most sacred places in Afghanistan and one of the most beautiful buildings in the Muslim world. The shrine was first built in the 1100s, because it was thought that Muhammad's heir, his cousin Ali, was buried there. The elegant mosque and minarets are covered in blue tile mosaics and painted tile panels.

Arts and Crafts

Afghanistan has a time-honored tradition of fine craftsmanship. From ancient potters and jewelry makers to glassblowers, woodworkers, and carpet weavers, skills have been passed down from generation to generation. Decades of war reduced the number of artisans who could afford materials to make their crafts. Likewise, there were fewer buyers. But times are changing. Universities and other schools are offering new art and craft classes. The classes are popular, and, contrary to tradition, many women are taking classes in painting, woodworking, jewelry making, photography, and calligraphy.

The village of Istalif in the foothills of the Hindu Kush has an ancient tradition of pottery making. The clay comes from nearby mountains. Potters transport the clay by donkey and

mix it with plants and water by stomping on the mixture barefoot. Istalifi potters are known for their beautiful natural glazes.

Every ethnic group, tribe, and clan has its own style of carpet weaving. Most Afghan carpets are wool and use rich natural dyes, usually dark red, brown, black, and tan, and sometimes light green or blue. Patterns are typically geometric. But some Afghan weavers have chosen to portray life during war. Afghan "war rugs" use traditional style and colors, but have images of tanks, rifles, helicopters, and exploding bombs.

Carpets woven by nomadic tribes are made to suit their lifestyle. The weavers raise and shear the sheep, collect and make the dyes, spin the wool into yarn, and weave using

A potter in Istalif works at a wheel.

looms tied to their bodies. Nomadic weavers do not make their carpets for sale. They make carpets for praying and to cover their walls and doorways. Afghan nomad weavers never sell a rug at market unless they have made a new one and no longer need the old one. Given the rarity of the rugs, they are highly sought after by collectors and museums.

Afghan war rugs incorporate images of tanks and guns.

Music

The music of Afghanistan is a diverse combination of Indian, Persian, Islamic, and Central Asian musical styles. Afghanistan's musical heritage includes components of Indian and Persian songs, classical Uzbek and Tajik compositions, Islamic chants and melodies, and folk music from many lands. Despite the diversity, much of the music is played with the same traditional musical instruments. Many types of drums are played, including the Persian *zerbaghali*, which is made of clay; the *tumbak*, a handheld wooden drum; and the *tabla*, a pair of small drums frequently played throughout South Asia. Common stringed instruments include the *dutar*, the *tambur*,

Homayoun Sakhi plays a rubab. Sakhi, who now lives in the United States, is considered one of the masters of the instrument.

and the *rubab*, the national instrument of Afghanistan. The rubab, an ancestor of the cello, has six strings and is carved of a single piece of wood from a mulberry or rosewood tree.

Afghanistan is also home to pop, rock, and rap performers. Farhad Darya is thought to be the first Afghan to write and perform a rock song. He has made more than thirty albums and has sponsored music festivals in Kabul. Some Afghan singers try for fame on a TV show called *Afghan Star*, which is much like *American Idol*. One of the most popular shows in Afghanistan, it has aired for more than a decade.

TV and Radio

TV and radio stations throughout Afghanistan broadcast music, news, religion, sports, dramas, comedies, and other forms of entertainment in Dari, Pashto, and local languages. Several stations stream their programs online. Afghanistan has more than four million internet users, and as electricity comes to more remote areas, the number of users rises.

Afghan filmmakers are known for their documentaries. New movie theaters are opening in the cities. Traditionally, only men went to movies, but that is slowly changing. In Kabul, there is a new theater for women and children. Indian movies are popular.

Literature

Poetry is the foremost literary form in Afghanistan. In 1010, a poet named Ferdowsi wrote "The Persian Book of Kings," an epic poem with fifty thousand rhyming couplets. He later

"Afghan Girl"

Mozhdah Jamalzadah is an Afghan singer, songwriter, and television personality. Born during the Afghan civil war, her family fled to Canada, where she studied journalism, philosophy, and political science. She composed a political song called "Dokhtare Afghan," meaning "Afghan Girl," and performed it at the White House for President Barack Obama. Jamalzadah returned to Afghanistan and became the host of a popular television talk show. She has received death threats from fundamentalist Muslims because of her discussions on controversial topics, such as the treatment of women and children in Afghanistan, but she continues to broadcast her show and perform music.

inspired other poets such as Sanai, from Ghazni, and Rumi, from Balkh. Rumi was a Sufi who wrote mystical, moral lines, such as "Every object, every being / is a jar full of delight."

Many of the most admired poets in Afghanistan today are women. As positive changes occur in the treatment of women, more women are speaking out. Khaledah Forugh, a professor of Persian literature at Kabul University, is a poet who has published many works of sadness, anger, and hope:

You who have not plucked / a single leaf from the tree of hope / will you ever / from the ocean of darkness / build a bridge to light?

Another well-known poet is Bahar Saeed, who expresses her resistance to conservative attitudes toward women:

This veil cannot conceal me, as my hair / its mere sight — will not paint me bare / I am Sun. I glimmer through curtain's cloth / It can't eclipse my light, not the darkest dark.

CHAPTER 10

Home, Friends, and Family

712

I N SOME PARTS OF AFGHANISTAN, LIFESTYLES HAVE
not changed for decades or even centuries. Village life is
simple, and customs have mostly remained the same. Life is
more varied for city dwellers. No matter their circumstances,
Afghans are deeply bonded to family and community. They
are social and visit one another often. Whether in city or
village, men gather in teahouses to talk, and women pride
themselves on hospitality offered to guests in their homes.

Opposite: **Women pose with their children in Mazar-i-Sharif.**

Village Life

Farming and herding families rise in the morning, wash,
pray, and then feed their cows, goats, and sheep. Afterward,

An Afghan family eats lunch sitting on the floor of their simple home in Kabul.

many men leave for jobs on farms or in shops. Others work as woodworkers, brickmakers, construction workers, and at other jobs. Women care for children and tend family gardens. Some women have jobs such as weaving, or doing other families' sewing and laundry. In some communities, such as Hazara, Tajik, Uzbek, and nomadic groups, women work alongside men, herding livestock and tending the fields.

Village homes are humble, often a small, single-story mud house. Rooms are furnished with mats, pillows, rugs, and mattresses. During the day, sleeping rugs, blankets, and mattresses are piled in the corner of the room. Each house has a *hujra*, or guest room, at the front. Guests are an important part of everyday life.

Opium Wars

Farmers in the Helmand Province have had their lives upended by war. Their land is ruined. Their fields are full of land mines, and their orchards have been burned to the ground. To return to farming, farmers need to borrow money to buy seed, farm equipment, and fertilizer for their soil. Often the only people willing to loan anything to the farmers are the Taliban and local warlords, who impose high fees and demand payment even if the harvest is small. As a result, many farmers resort to growing opium poppies, which grow easily and reliably. The poppies are used to produce opium, a highly addictive drug. It is estimated that 90 percent of the world's opium is grown in Afghanistan. When it is harvest time, the Taliban and the warlords join farmers to harvest the opium and collect fees and taxes. Then they use the money to buy more guns and other weapons.

Many villages do not have electricity, so people cook and heat their homes with wood or charcoal. Some people have oil and gas-powered generators, but they are very expensive to operate. Many people rely on candles and oil lamps for lighting at night. Not every village has running water. But many villages have community wells.

City Life

Most of Afghanistan's population lives in Kabul and other cities. War has affected the southern cities such as Helmand and Kandahar the most. Many refugees have moved to the cities without money, work, or education. Buildings, roads, and bridges have been battered by war. There are too few schools and jobs. Neighborhoods of tiny homes are expanding rapidly as the population swells.

More northerly cities such as Kabul, Mazar-i-Sharif, and Herat are faring better. Kabul is crowded but exciting. There are new shops, restaurants, theaters, museums, and parks. Over the last decade, many professionals—doctors, nurses, teachers, bankers, and businesspeople—fled the country to escape war. But as the new government has become stable, many are returning. More young people are attending college. New professional jobs are opening up. Carpenters, plumbers,

A teenager in Kabul displays a henna design on her hand. People in Kabul and other cities tend to be less traditional than those in the countryside.

brickmakers, and electricians can barely keep up with the demand for new houses and the need to rebuild damaged buildings and roads. More urban homes now have electricity and running water.

A grandmother shops with her grandchild at a market in Mazar-i-Sharif. Afghanistan has one of the lowest life expectancies of any country in the world, at just fifty-one years.

The Family

Afghan families are often large, commonly with five or more children. In most rural families, children, parents, cousins, aunts and uncles, and grandparents live close to one another, frequently in the same house or family compound. Family members have different roles in different ethnic groups, but in most families, men are the head of the household, and the greatest respect goes to the eldest man.

Mothers, aunts, and grandmothers all help raise the children. Women take care of the home and tend gardens. Because

A young Afghan boy
works at a biscuit factory.

of the many years of war, many men have died or become disabled, so they can no longer support the family. Especially in conservative communities, women are not supposed to work outside the home. Extended family members help financially when they can, but frequently children must work to help feed their family. About 25 percent of Afghan children work full or part time. Laws prohibit children younger than fourteen to work, but in times of great need, that law is ignored. Children have jobs such as brickmaking, weaving, collecting garbage, or finding objects that can be sold or recycled. Others sell fruit or bread in the marketplace or collect wood and bits of debris to take home to fuel the family's stove.

Family Traditions

Afghans follow centuries-old rituals to celebrate births and weddings, as well as to honor those who have died.

Wedding Halls

An Afghan wedding is a huge event. The entire family of both the bride and the groom come together to celebrate.

In big cities, wedding guests can number in the hundreds or even thousands. As one groom explained, "I invited my cousins; my cousins' cousins; my neighbors; also people who live in the surrounding areas; and, of course, people from my village, and 100 to 150 colleagues." Many wedding couples have no idea who all their guests are. Hospitality knows no bounds to an Afghan, so whenever there is a celebration, no one, invited or not, is turned away. Passersby often stop at weddings to enjoy the celebration.

Huge wedding halls abound in cities. They are colorful, brightly lit, and inviting. In Kabul, especially, weddings can cost more than a year's salary. Even poor families will go into debt to pay for clothes,

food, musicians, flowers, and photography. Young men sometimes put off getting married because they cannot afford the ceremony. Weddings have grown so expensive that parliament passed a law limiting the number of guests in a wedding hall to five hundred people.

Before a child is born, the father's mother prepares a meal for female friends and family. The mother's mother brings gifts as well as herbal folk medicine. In rural areas, once a child is born, men go outside the new parents' house and shoot off rifles. The father or a grandfather whispers the call to prayer into the baby's ear. The father's family prepares gifts of dried fruit for well-wishers who visit.

Traditionally, families arrange marriages for their children. In some more liberal communities, the future bride or groom can reject the choice. Weddings last days. On the first day, the bride and her female friends and relatives gather for a henna party. Henna is a natural vegetable dye that is used to decorate the bride's skin. The groom's family sends children to deliver henna to the bride. On the wedding day, the bride and her female family members visit a salon and dress.

Meanwhile, the groom and his male family and friends have a large lunch and are entertained by musicians. After his celebration, the groom leads a procession to the bride's home. There, a speech is given about marriage. Then the couple sits on a sofa under a shawl. They are given a mirror and a copy of the Qur'an. They look into the mirror and see themselves for the first time as a married couple. Then they read passages of the Qur'an together before everyone relaxes with music, good food, and dancing.

When an Afghan dies, his or her family washes the body to purify the soul. People are supposed to be buried within twenty-four hours. In villages, bodies are buried simply, without any markers. Wealthier people engrave tombstones with verses from the Qur'an.

Clothing

Many Afghans wear traditional clothing. Garments are made of cotton, wool, and sometimes silk. They are often embroidered and colorful. Women typically wear loose pants along with an overdress. They wear a scarf called a *chador*, which wraps around the neck and covers the head. In conservative communities, women wear a *burka*, a garment that covers the body, head, and face.

Traditional menswear is called a *shalwar kamiz*. It is a pair of loose drawstring pants and a long, loose-fitting shirt. Some men

also wear an embroidered vest, or shawl. Men of the Central Asian ethnic groups wear belts or sashes and wool or felt hats, which are usually embroidered. Pashtun men usually wear a turban. Hazara men often wear a rolled headscarf.

In many places, men now wear Western dress such as jeans and fitted shirts. Professional women often wear a Western-style blouse, a long skirt, and a chador.

Food and Drink

Afghan cuisine blends influences from India, Iran, the Middle East, and other regions. Meat is a main ingredient in the Afghan diet. Kebabs, which are chunks of meat skewered onto sticks and roasted over flames, are an everyday meal. Rice and handmade noodles are the staple ingredients of dishes, which feature curries made with chicken, lamb, and beef. Thick sauces are spiced with cardamom, cumin, mint, garlic, and saffron. A typical meal called *qabili palao* is a casserole made with browned rice, lamb, carrots, raisins, and pistachios. Favorite vegetables are spinach, red pepper, and eggplant. Afghan desserts smell as sweet as they taste. A favorite is a custard with cardamom, pistachios, and a touch of rose water.

In many homes, people eat sitting on the floor on pillows or rugs. Families share breakfast and dinner together, but many villagers do not stop for lunch. Instead, they carry dried fruits and nuts with them for energy. Tea, usually green tea, is drunk all day.

Holidays

Many Afghan holidays are religious. Those that are not include Independence Day, Labor Day, and Nowruz, or New Year. Nowruz celebrations can last for days. On Nowruz, people celebrate by wearing new clothes, cleaning and making repairs to their house, and giving a fresh coat of paint to buildings and garden walls. Girls and women henna their hands and visit shrines to pray. The most time-honored Nowruz tradition is to forgive mistakes. Evenings are spent feasting and visiting with friends and family. During the day, there are flower festivals and games.

Eid al-Fitr is a joyful religious holiday. It celebrates the end of Ramadan, a month of fasting. The feasting begins after morning prayers. Women shop for days buying fruits and nuts and other special foods in preparation for the holiday. Families gather to eat and visit friends and extended family. Children go knocking on doors, wishing people a happy Eid. They are rewarded with treats from women and money from men.

Fun and Sports

Afghans enjoy games and sports. The traditional national sport is *buzkashi*, which means "grab the goat." The game is played by teams of men on horseback. The first team to pick up and drag a goat carcass past the other team's goal line and back again wins.

Flying fighter kites is a popular activity in Afghanistan. People make their own kites out of paper and bamboo, and attach wire and ground-up glass to the string. They then battle other kites, trying to cut the opposing kite loose from its string.

Boys fly plastic bags as kites from a high wall in Kabul.

Afghanistan's first professional women's soccer league was established in 2014.

Kite flyers usually pair up to form a team. While one player steers the kite and runs up hillsides or climbs on rooftops to attack other kites, the other player runs and collects the kites that have been cut loose. The last kite flying wins.

Afghan men and boys have long played soccer. Since the fall of the Taliban, girls and women have begun enjoying the sport. Girls generally play indoors or behind walls, out of view from the public. But there are both men's and women's Afghan national soccer teams that compete internationally. In 2016, the women's team got new uniforms made of stretchy athletic fabric. But in keeping with Muslim customs, the uniforms cover the players from head to ankle.

Cricket, a sport somewhat like baseball that the British introduced into Afghanistan, is becoming the country's favorite sport. Afghanistan's national team has been ranked one of the top ten teams in the world.

Health and Education

During years of war and the Taliban's rise to power, Afghanistan's health care system fell apart. War, poverty, and lack of good

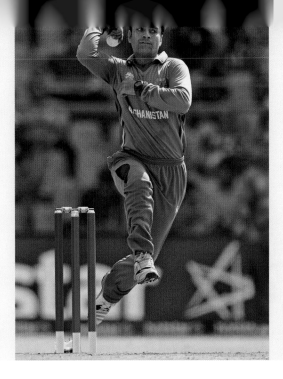

nutrition caused people a lot of serious health problems, in addition to which there was a lack of medical clinics and health care workers. Many doctors, nurses, and medical technicians fled the country. Hundreds of clinics were forced to close. Women and girls particularly suffered because there were so few women doctors and women were not allowed to see male doctors. Since the fall of the Taliban, much has improved. Health clinics are opening in villages and towns. Today, about 60 percent of Afghans live within an hour's walk of a clinic or hospital.

The Taliban also did great harm to the nation's education. The Taliban shut down all schools for girls because they did not believe women should be educated. Many Afghan parents tried to educate their girls in secret, sending them to underground schools. Since the fall of the Taliban, the education system has improved dramatically, although many children still cannot attend school.

College students attend a class in Kabul. Education for Afghan women has made great strides in recent years. As much as 90 percent of middle-aged women received no education at all.

Not all villages have a school. Instead, many classes are held in tents, houses, or under trees. In many schools, there are 40 to 45 students for every teacher. Most schools are overcrowded and must hold classes in two or three shifts. Literacy, meaning the percentage of people over fifteen years old who can read and write, is only 24 percent for females and 52 percent for males. But as more support is coming to build schools, train teachers, and include girls in education, people hope literacy rates will rise quickly. Not so long ago, many girls, if they went to school at all, left school as young teenagers to get married. But in Kabul today, more than 40 percent of high school students are female. Many people believe the education system is making great strides.

The First Lady

Rula Ghani became the first lady of Afghanistan when her husband, Ashraf Ghani, became president in 2014. She studied at the American University of Beirut and Columbia University in New York, earning degrees in political science. Since becoming a public figure in Afghanistan, she has been a strong advocate for women's rights. She is careful not to offend conservative groups, saying, "I can talk in some places freely, but not in others." However, that has not stood in her way. She encourages social change, saying, "The women of Afghanistan must have the courage to talk about it. They should raise their voice to say they don't like it and they won't accept it."

Ghani has been behind the creation of the first women's university in Afghanistan. The school is a major first step in providing higher education to women. It is needed because many conservative Muslims do not allow their daughters to attend a college with men.

The college, called Moraa Educational Complex, offers programs in medicine, science, technology, fine arts, and business. Ghani spoke at the opening ceremony in 2016, saying, "If I've achieved a higher respect for women and for their role in society then I would be very happy. That would really be my greatest wish."

Looking Ahead

Afghanistan is a country with longstanding problems. War and terrorism are part of everyday life in many parts of the country, including the capital city of Kabul. But the desire of people to improve their lives is strong. More people, especially women, are finding their voices and making demands on their government to improve living conditions. They want electricity, clean water, employment opportunities, and education for all. Given the government's desire for change, the nation's bountiful natural resources, and the strength and fortitude of its citizens, many people are hopeful that life in Afghanistan will get better.

Timeline

	AFGHAN HISTORY		WORLD HISTORY	

AFGHAN HISTORY		WORLD HISTORY	
Dost Muhammad becomes the leader of Afghanistan.	1826		
Russia and Britain vie for power in the region in what is called the Great Game.	1838–1907		
		The American Civil War ends.	1865
		The first practical lightbulb is invented.	1879
The Durand Line establishes the border between Afghanistan and today's Pakistan.	1893	World War I begins.	1914
Afghanistan declares independence from Great Britain.	1919	The Bolshevik Revolution brings communism to Russia.	1917
		A worldwide economic depression begins.	1929
Mohammed Zahir Shah becomes the last Afghan king.	1933	World War II begins.	1939
		World War II ends.	1945
		Humans land on the Moon.	1969
Mohammad Daud Khan declares himself president.	1973	The Vietnam War ends.	1975
The Soviet Union invades Afghanistan.	1979		
The Soviets withdraw from Afghanistan.	1989	The Berlin Wall is torn down as communism crumbles in Eastern Europe.	1989
The Taliban gains control of much of the country.	Mid-1990s	The Soviet Union breaks into separate states.	1991
The Taliban destroys the Bamiyan Buddhas; the United States and its allies topple the Taliban government.	2001	Terrorists attack the World Trade Center in New York City and the Pentagon near Washington, D.C.	2001
Hamid Karzai is chosen president in free elections; a new constitution is adopted.	2004	A tsunami in the Indian Ocean destroys coastlines in Africa, India, and Southeast Asia.	2004
		The United States elects its first African American president.	2008
President Ashraf Ghani and CEO Abdullah Abdullah share power in the National Unity Government.	2014	Donald Trump is elected U.S. president.	2016

Fast Facts

Official name: Islamic Republic of Afghanistan

Capital: Kabul

Official languages: Pashto and Dari

Kabul

National flag

Koh-i-Baba Mountains

Official religion:	Islam
Type of government:	Democracy
Head of government:	President
Head of state:	President
Area:	251,827 square miles (652,230 sq km)
Bordering nations:	China, Tajikistan, Uzbekistan, and Turkmenistan to the north; Iran to the west; Pakistan to the east
Highest elevation:	Mount Nowshakh, 24,580 feet (7,492 m) above sea level
Lowest elevation:	Amu Darya riverbed, 846 feet (258 m) above sea level
Longest river entirely within Afghanistan:	Helmand River, about 715 miles (1,150 km)
Average daily high temperature:	In Kabul, 38°F (3°C) in January, 89°F (32°C) in July; in Kandahar, 42°F (6°C) in January, 105°F (41°C) in July
Average daily low temperature:	In Kabul, 16°F (−9°C) in January, 59°F (15°C) in July; in Kandahar, 31°F (−1°C) in January, 73°F (23°C) in July
Average annual precipitation:	12 inches (30 cm)

Friday Mosque

National population (2012 est.): 33,332,025

Population of major cities (2013 est.):

Kabul	3,589,000
Kandahar	491,500
Herat	436,300
Mazar-i-Sharif	368,100
Kunduz	304,600

Landmarks:
- ▶ *Blue Mosque,* Mazar-i Sharif
- ▶ *Friday Mosque,* Herat
- ▶ *Mousallah Complex,* Herat
- ▶ *National Museum of Afghanistan,* Kabul
- ▶ *Wakhan National Park,* Wakhan Corridor

Economy: Afghanistan's major agricultural products include wheat, rice, cotton, grapes, melons, and nuts. The nation has rich deposits of copper, salt, and chromium, as well as rubies, topaz, emeralds, and lapis lazuli. Many Afghans are involved in rearing goats, sheep, cattle, horses, and yaks. Manufactured products include processed food, fertilizers, pharmaceuticals, and crafts, such as carpet making and furniture making. In addition, goods made from animals such as shoes, bags, saddles, and wool are produced in Afghanistan.

Currency

Currency: Afghani. In 2017, 67 afghanis equaled US$1.

System of weights and measures: Metric system

Literacy rate: 24% women; 52% men

Schoolchildren

Rashid Khan

Common Afghan words and phrases:

PASHTO	DARI	ENGLISH
Salaam aalaikum	Salaam aalaikum	Hello
Senga yee?	Chetor aste?	How are you?
Mehrabani	Lotfan	Please
Manana	Tashakor	Thank you

Prominent Afghans:

Kamal ud-Din Behzad (ca. 1455–ca. 1536)
Artist

Farhad Darya (1962–)
Singer and composer

Ahmad Shah Durrani (ca. 1725–ca. 1773)
Founder of the Durrani dynasty

Shamsia Hassani (1988–)
Artist

Rashid Khan (1998–)
Cricket player

Ahmad Shah Massoud (1953–2001)
Leader of the Northern Alliance

Rumi (1207–1273)
Poet

Mohammed Zahir (1914–2007)
Last king of Afghanistan

To Find Out More

Books

▶ Ali-Karamali, Sumbul. *Growing Up Muslim: Understanding Islamic Beliefs and Practices*. New York: Delacorte Press, 2012.

▶ Ellis, Deborah. *Kids of Kabul: Living Bravely Through a Never-ending War*. Berkeley, CA: Groundwood Books/House of Anansi Press, 2012.

▶ Kavanaugh, Dorothy. *War in Afghanistan: Overthrow of the Taliban and Aftermath*. Broomall, PA: Mason Crest Publishers, 2016.

Videos

▶ *Families of Afghanistan*. Cincinnati: Master Communications, 2010.

▶ *Ramadan: A Fast of Faith*. New York: Films Media Group, 2013.

▶ Visit this Scholastic website for more information on Afghanistan:
www.factsfornow.scholastic.com
Enter the keyword **Afghanistan**

Index

Page numbers in *italics* indicate illustrations.

Bactrian Empire, 40–41, *40*
cabinet ministers, 66, 84
communism, 56
conservation, 28, 35
constitution, 64, 67, 71, 84
coup, 55
Daud Khan, 55–56
Dost Muhammad, 50, 51
elections, 57, 60–61, 66, 68
employment in, 80
executive branch, 57, 58, 60, 64, 66, 70, *70*, 84, 127
Ghaznavid Empire, 46
Great Game, 51–52
Habibullah Khan, 53
Hamid Karzai, 57
Hephthalite Empire, 46, *46*
House of Elders, 68
House of the People, 68, 71
independence, 64
Islamic religion and, 64
jirga council, 71
judicial branch, 70, 71
Kushan Empire, *41*, 43–46
legislative branch, *62*, 66
loya jirga (grand council), 49–50, 60, 71, *71*
Macedonian Empire, 41–42, *41*, *42*
Mauryan dynasty, *41*, 42–43
military, 56
Moghul Empire, 49, 50
Mohammad Omar, 58
Mohammed Zahir, 133
Mongol Empire, 48–49
Muhammad Nadir Shah, 54
National Assembly, 66, 68, 69
National Environmental Protection Agency, 35
National Museum and, 103
Northern Alliance, 57
presidents, 84, 127
Safavid Empire, 49

Sasanian Empire, 46, *46*
Sharia law, 58
shura meetings, 69
Supreme Court, 71
Taliban, 57
tree smuggling and, 28
unity government, 61
weddings and, 119
women and, 68, 87
Zahir Shah, 54–55
graffiti, 104–105, *104*
grasses, 29
Great Britain, 51–52, *52*, 64, 124
Great Mosque of Herat, 25, *25*, 79, 105–106, *105*
Greek language, 45
green tea, 122
gross domestic product (GDP), 80
Gujar people, 84, 88

H
Habibullah Khan, 53
Hadith (Islamic holy book), 95
hajj (fifth pillar of Islam), 99
Hari Rud River, 20–21
Hassani, Shamsia, *104*, 133
Hazara people, 58, 84, 87, 88, 91, 114, 121
health care, 61, 124–125
Helmand Province, 115
Helmand River, 18, 20, 21
henna, *116*, 119–120, 122
Hephthalite Empire, 46, *46*
Herat. *See also* cities.
    Ahmad Shah Durrani and, 50
    Alexander the Great in, 41
    art in, 103
    education in, 87
    employment in, 87
    Great Mosque, 105–106, *105*
    Hazara people in, 87
    Islam and, 47

literature in, 103
Mongol Empire in, 48, 49
Mousallah Complex, 105
population of, 25, 88
Safavid Empire in, 49
Hinduism, 47, 90, 98
Hindu Kush, 19, 20, 21, 29, 43, 46, 65, 84
historical maps. *See also* maps.
    Early Afghanistan, *41*
    Later Empires, *46*
holidays
    national, 122
    religious, 97, 99, 122
House of Elders, 68
House of the People, 68, 71
housing, 39, 81, 114–115, 122
hydroelectric power, 21, 81

I
imports, 81
independence, 53, 55, 64
Independence Day, 122
Indian Premier League (IPL), 125, *125*
Indus Valley Civilization, 39, *39*, 40, *41*
insect life, 33
internet, 110
irrigation, 20, 21, 22
Islamic religion. *See also* religion.
    art and, 104
    Balkh and, 47
    Blue Mosque, 25, *25*
    communism and, 56
    Eid al-Fitr holiday, 122
    Five Pillars of Islam, 97–99
    government and, 64
    Great Mosque of Herat, 79
    Hadith (holy book), 95
    Herat and, 47
    holidays, 97, 99, 122
    Mahmud of Ghazni, 47

pottery, 39, 106–107, *107*
poverty, 35, 73
Presidential Palace, 65, *70*, 103
presidents, 55, 59, 60–61, 64, 66, 66,
    68, 69, 71, 84, 127
Pyanj River, 20
Pyanj Valley, 20

Q

qabili palao (national dish), 121–122,
    121
al-Qaeda terrorist group, 60
Qalat, *42*
Qizilbash people, 84, 88, 90
Qur'an (Islamic holy book), 94, 95, 97,
    103, 120

R

radio, 110, 125
Ramadan (Islamic holy month), 97,
    99, 122
refugees, 13, 90
Reg-i-Ruwan singing dune, 22
Registan Desert, 23
religion. *See also* Islamic religion.
    art and, 102–103
    Buddhism, 43, 46–47, *47*, 77, 98,
        102–103, *102*
    Christianity, 93, 94, 98
    Hinduism, 47, 90, 98
    Judaism, 94
    Sikhism, 98
reptilian life, 33–34, *34*
rice, 121
roadways, 12, 14, *15*, 28, 61, 79, 115
Royesh, Aziz, 87
rubab (musical instrument), *109*
Rumi, 111, 133
Russia, 51, 52, 91
Russian tortoises, 34, *34*

S

Saeed, Bahar, 111
Safavid Empire, 49
saffron, 74, *75*
saiga antelope, 31, *31*
Sakhi, Homayoun, *109*
salat (second pillar of Islam), 97–98
sandstorms, *24*
Sasanian Empire, 46, *46*
sawm (third pillar of Islam), 98
scouts, 14–15
scrub brush, 29
sculpture, 102, *103*
September 11 attacks, 60
service industries, 80, *80*
shahadah (first pillar of Islam), 97
Shahrak, 18
shalwar kamiz (clothing), 120
Sharia law, 58
Shi'a Muslims, 87, 90, 95, 96, 98
Shortughai, 39
Shrine of Hazrat Ali. *See* Blue Mosque.
shura meetings, 69
Siberian cranes, 33, *33*
Sikhism, 98
silk, *78*, 120
Silk Road, 44–46, *44*, 49, 101
singing sand dunes, 22, *22*
snakes, 34
snow leopards, 30, *30*, 32
soccer, 124, *124*
solar energy, 81
Soraya, queen of Afghanistan, 55
Soviet-Afghan War, 56–57, *56*
Soviet Union, 12, 14–15, 52, 53, 55,
    56, *56*, 57, 58, 87
sports, 124, *124*, *133*
steppe region, 22, 26, 29, 30–31, 33, 76
Sufi Muslims, 96
Sufism, 95–96, *96*
Sunni Muslims, 90, 95, 98
Supreme Court, 71

T

Tajik people, 57, 58, 84, 85–86, *85*, 88,
    91, 109, 114
Taliban, 14, 15, 57, 58, 60, 69, 71, 87,
    103, 104, 115, 124–125
tea, 122
television, 110, 125
textile industry, 25, *78*, 79
theater, 110
tiles, *105*, 106
Timur, leader of Mongol Empire, 49
Tomb of Hazrat Ali, 25
tortoises, 34, *34*
towns. *See also* cities; villages.
    Cyrus the Great and, 40
    health care, 125
    Qalat, *42*
    warfare and, 12
trade, 25, 37, 39, 41, 44–46, *44*
transportation, 14, *15*, *21*, 25, 53, 90
trees, 28, *28*, 29
tulip (national flower), 29
tumbak (musical instrument), 109
Turkmen people, 84, 88, *88*

U

United States, 55–56, 60, 61, 111
Uzbek people, 58, 84, 88, *88*, 109, 114

V

villages. *See also* cities; towns.
    agriculture, 113–114
    daily life, 113–114
    health care, 125
    housing, 114–115
    Istalif, 106–107, *107*
    shura meetings, 69
volcanoes, 19, 21

W

Wakhan Corridor, 20, 31, 35, *35*, 76,
    89, *89*

Meet the Author

RUTH BJORKLUND GREW UP IN RURAL New England where she went hiking, rowing, and sailing. She left New England, traveled, and eventually settled in Seattle, Washington, where she attended the University of Washington. There, she earned a bachelor's degree in comparative literature and a master's degree in library and information science.

She has been a children's and young adult librarian and has written many books on a wide range of subjects, including the history, geography, and culture of states and countries, health, endangered animals, and contemporary issues.

Today, Bjorklund lives on Bainbridge Island, a ferry ride away from Seattle. She enjoys kayaking, sailing, camping, and traveling. She has visited Southeast Asia, central Asia, China, Peru, Italy, Croatia, Canada, Mexico, and all fifty states. While traveling in the Pamir Mountains near Afghanistan, she was warmly welcomed by the Kyrgyz and Wakhi nomads of the region.

Photo Credits